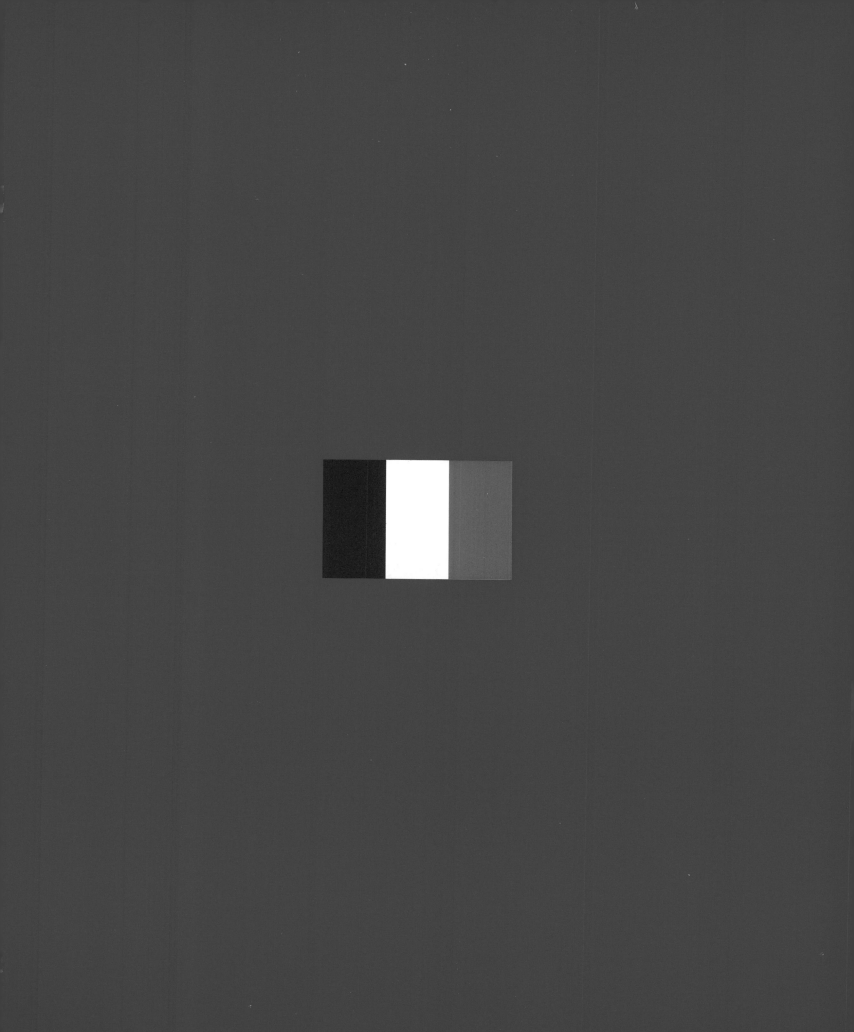

FR

PHILIP JODIDIO

ARCHITECTURE
IN FRANCE

TASCHEN

HONG KONG KÖLN LONDON LOS ANGELES MADRID PARIS TOKYO

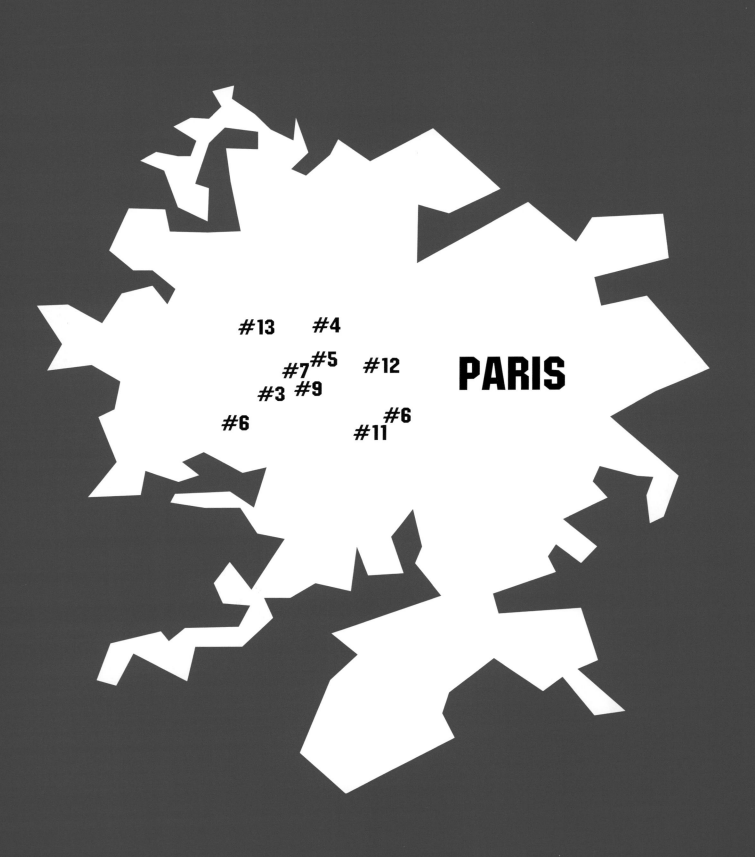

INTRODUCTION

DESPERATELY SEEKING DESCARTES

Cartesian? The French say they are. René Descartes (1596–1650) was the founder of analytic geometry and also of 17th-century rationalism, but he may be best known for the phrase "Cogito ergo sum" (I think therefore I am). An overview of contemporary French architecture certainly reveals a lot of thinking, a wealth of complex forms that seems to defy easy classification. What is clear is that trends like the minimalism seen in the work of English architects John Pawson or David Chipperfield has had a difficult time crossing the English Channel (or La Manche, as the French say). At the other extreme, French architects certainly aren't as enamored of extravagant computer-driven forms as the nearby Dutch, but it was in France that Lars Spuybroek of NOX was able to build his Maison-Folie (Lille-Wazemmes, 2001). What other country would select cutting-edge Japanese architects to build new structures for the Pompidou Center (Shigeru Ban, Metz) or the Louvre (SANAA, Sejima+Nishizawa, Lens)? In the past 25 years, France has called on foreign architects for high-profile projects, such as the Louvre Pyramid (I. M. Pei), the Bastille Opera (Carlos Ott) or the Grande Arche de la Défense (Johann Otto von Spreckelsen). The Mitterrand years (1981–95) did a great deal to reveal native talents at the same time as these major projects (Grands Travaux) were being carried out. Jean Nouvel with his Institut du Monde Arabe on the Seine in Paris, Christian de Portzamparc (Cité de la Musique, Paris) and Dominique Perrault (French National Library) all came to public attention thanks to the substantial resources lavished by the government on these new facilities. Another trend emerged almost simultaneously with the rise to notoriety of interior or furniture designers like Philippe Starck or Jean-Michel Wilmotte, who worked closely with Pei on the museum design in the Louvre. Both of these figures have also delved into architecture with some success. More recently, a new generation of designers, a number of whom were initially trained by Starck's office, has emerged on the international stage, at the point of juncture between design and architecture. Patrick Jouin and Matali Crasset are in this category. With ups and downs often related to economic considerations and varying degrees of government intervention, France has thus succeeded in maintaining a vibrant architectural culture while opening its borders to outside designers more than most other developed countries. The architects featured in this book were selected on the basis of their recent work and in an attempt to give an overview of current styles and methods. They vary in age from their early 40s (Matali Crasset or Manuelle Gautrand) to their early 60s (Jean-Paul Viguier or Denis Valode), but also in the scale and nature of their work. Christian de Portzamparc, winner of the 1994 Pritzker Prize, and Jean Nouvel are considered major figures on the international architectural scene, while others, such as Jean-Marie Duthilleul, head architect of the French National Railways (SNCF), are not as well known to the general public despite having had a considerable impact on the public in France and abroad. Small offices are contrasted here with large corporate-style teams like Valode & Pistre.

COLOR IS LIFE

Despite the variety of the work presented here, it may be that the rational, analytic character identified with Descartes can be discerned in the ambitions or methods of these architects. Born in 1965 in Châlon-en-Champage, Matali Crasset studied at the École Nationale Supérieure de Création Industrielle in Paris, working afterwards with Philippe Starck and Thomson Multimedia before creating her own office in Paris in 1998. "The French are scared of color," she declares, sitting at a long table in her atelier-home, in the Belleville district of Paris. There is no shortage of pastel shades here, nor in her work in general. "I really don't believe that a cheerful environment has to be reserved for children," she says with an assurance that is reflected in work such as her Hi Hotel in Nice. Crasset affirms that "Color is life." She explains her ideas in terms of currents and feelings rather than the more utilitarian approach of many traditional architects. In the end this is her most radical departure from the current norms in architecture and design. And it seems as if her call to re-evaluate the functions of design has been heard. Whether via teaching at design schools in Copenhagen, Milan, Lausanne and Amsterdam, or participating in the recent Beijing architecture Biennale with a custom-designed apartment or in a major Franco-Chinese exhibition in Shanghai, Crasset's name and influence has now spread well beyond France. Like her former mentor Starck, Matali Crasset sees no limits to her own creativity. She has set out to redefine or perhaps to erase the boundaries between design and architecture. Work on breaking down the barriers between architecture and other disciplines such as art or design is going forward in many countries, but Crasset represents a particularly French approach, imbued with a spirit of gentle revolt and an intelligent analysis of what is wrong with modern space.

Odile Decq is another prominent woman on the French architectural scene. The former partner of Benoît Cornette, who passed away in 1998, she has recently come to international attention with her topographically inspired project for the Liaunig Museum in Neuhaus, Austria. In France, her design for the FRAC Bretagne, one of a series of contemporary art facilities in the country, combines an exciting appearance with a functional efficiency. Like Crasset, Odile Decq has made a point of creating a signature style not only in her architecture, but also in her physical appearance. Her extravagant hair arrangements and make-up definitely set her apart, but she has amply proven that women can have a place in the French architectural system, despite the clear dominance of her male counterparts.

LEARNING TO FLY HIGH

The "punk" look is definitely not Jean-Marie Duthilleul's thing. A brilliant graduate of the elite Polytechnique school, an engineer and an architect, Duthilleul has done more to redefine rail transport in France and elsewhere than any other living architect. As head architect of the SNCF he has been responsible not only for modernizing such venerable stations as the Gare du Nord or the Gare Montparnasse in Paris, but also for creating a series of new stations for north or southbound TGV lines. In a somewhat more understated style than Santiago Calatrava, Duthilleul has refashioned the railway station to make it a pleasant place to be, where light and soaring spaces are the rule rather than the exception. Duthilleul's technical mastery and his association with the powerful French railway monopoly has allowed him to branch out in recent years, working in China and several other countries. He has also been able to carry out a number of other projects, including office buildings and religious structures, such as the church published in this book.

Manuelle Gautrand, born in 1961, came into view abruptly in France when she was included in the selection of architects participating in François Pinault's competition for a new museum of contemporary art. What made her stand out was that she held her own in the presence of Tadao Ando, Steven Holl, Rem Koolhaas, Dominique Perrault, MVRDV and Álvaro Siza. Aside from her projects for the Administrative Center of Saint-Étienne and the expansion and renovation of the Lille Museum of Modern Art, Gautrand has undertaken an extremely visible project in Paris. The car manufacturer Citroën installed a showroom at number 42, Champs-Élysées, in 1927. In 1931, the firm called on its factory designer Ravazé and its art director Pierre Louys to redo the building in a style judged befitting of the brand until 1984. Home to a restaurant for the next years, the Citroën showroom had become outdated when the company decided in 2002 to organize an international design competition with such participants as Zaha Hadid, Daniel Libeskind and Christian de Portzamparc. The winner was Manuelle Gautrand, who rebuilt the 1200 square-meter structure entirely. Using the inverted double-V symbol of the firm, Gautrand designed a complex glass façade that reveals successive platforms where Citroën vehicles are to be exhibited. She makes subtle reference to the previous Art-Deco façade of the showroom that was so long admired. The platform system permits full use of the considerable interior height while not actually breaking up the space. In her ability to face up to the "heavy-weight" names of international architecture and to undertake complex projects, Gautrand has evolved toward a subtle modernity that is neither derivative nor entirely groundbreaking. She may be the most attractive face of French Cartesianism.

Dominique Jakob and Brendan MacFarlane do not form the most typically French firm in this group. Jakob is French, but MacFarlane was born in New Zealand and the pair met in the office of Morphosis in Los Angeles. From their sophisticated "blob" forms in the Georges Restaurant at the Pompidou Center in Paris (2000), to their subtle and intelligent reworking of the apartment of the art collector Daniel Bosser, this dynamic couple has shown an ability to adapt to different situations, and to remain resolutely modern, even when working in the context of an Haussmann-style apartment or an old automobile factory (Renault International Communication Center, Boulogne, 2005). With others, like Gautrand, they certainly represent the rising generation of French architecture.

THREE WAYS TO WIN THE GAME

Jean Nouvel hardly needs to be presented to those who follow contemporary architecture. A glance at his list of recent projects says a great deal about his international standing. His phallic Agbar Tower set on Barcelona's thoroughfare the Diagonal was inaugurated on September 16, 2005. Ten days later, his extension of the Reina Sofia contemporary art center opened to critical acclaim. As he completed a 44-story tower in Qatar and an apartment building in SoHo in New York, Nouvel completed the most significant new building erected in France in many years, the Museum of Arts and Civilizations on the quai Branly in Paris. Four days after the June opening of the museum, he was in Minneapolis for the inauguration of the Guthrie Theater. Nouvel does not leave critics or the public indifferent. Whereas his undeniable originality and the strength of his architecture cannot be denied, he does challenge public perceptions of modern architecture. The elevated, reptilian volume of the Quai Branly Museum is, according to its maker, "unlike anything ever seen in the West." Though modesty may not be his main quality in this instance, Nouvel is right to underline the fact that he has broken with almost every convention of contemporary architecture with this project.

In an entirely different style together with Shigeru Ban/Jean de Gastines, Anne Lacaton and Jean-Philippe Vassal, Duncan Lewis, Scape Architecture + Block and Art'M Architecture, Nouvel undertook to design one of the more remarkable groups of social housing seen in France for many years. With its prominence as an industrial center rising in the mid-1880s, the eastern city of Mulhouse launched a workers' housing area with 200 residences at the edge of the city, under the authority of the Société mulhousienne des cités ouvrières. The average size of the houses, 47 m^2, was considered generous at the time, but became a problem in later years. A promoter, Pierre Zemp (SOMCO), contacted Jean Nouvel in 2000 and asked him to work on new housing, inspired by the tradition of the Cité Manifeste as it was called. The planned site, l'îlot Schoettlé, is situated at the edge of the historic Cité ouvrière. Nouvel brought the other participants together for the promoter in 2001. An overall construction budget of €6 229 600 was allotted at the time for the 60 planned residences. As the promoter points out, despite the different styles of the architects involved—the projects of Nouvel and Lacaton & Vassal are published in this volume—all of their work tends to render boundaries less distinct—to create openings and a transition between interior and exterior that is as indistinguishable as possible given the local climate. Perhaps a bit harsh in appearance, the social housing involved set standards of space, light and quality that are rare in France, a tribute to Jean Nouvel and the other architects involved.

Dominque Perrault was vaulted from relative obscurity to architectural stardom when a jury presided by I. M. Pei selected him to design the last and perhaps most difficult of the Grands Travaux, the French National Library in the 13th arrondissement in Paris. Originally designed as a set of four open books, each 100 meters high, the library saw its height reduced in an intense controversy. Perrault's tough modernism, often dressed in metal mesh, remains as uncompromising as it was in 1989 when he started work on the library. He focuses on modern art and has a decidedly "anti-modern" tendency to dig his buildings into the earth, as he did with the Olympic Velodrome, Swimming and Diving Pool (Berlin, Germany, 1992-99). The most apt artistic comparison for his toughness might be Richard Serra's large-scale Corten steel sculptures. Perrault takes risks, sometimes willfully designing outside of the accepted norms, as he did with the library. But does its layout correspond as well to the function of lending and reading books as it might? Revolt, too, is part of the French personality and Perrrault, together with Rudy Ricciotti, incarnates this aspect of the country's architectural creativity.

Christian de Portzamparc, an influential presence in architecture, both through his own buildings and his master plans such as that of the avenue de France, behind Perrault's library, is the only French winner of the Pritzker Prize. With buildings such as the LVMH Tower on 57th Street in Manhattan, or the music center he is currently building in Rio, Portzamparc has done more to carry his country's colors abroad than almost any other living architect aside from Nouvel. His modernism is decidedly lyrical, with some exceptions, such as the rather heavy French Embassy on the Pariser Platz in Berlin. In Rio, he will show his fundamental admiration for the flights of the imagination rendered in concrete by Oscar Niemeyer. His drawings and watercolors reveal the artistic background of his work, but the real underpinning of his architecture is what permits him to avoid easy classification. The lyrical modernism of the late LeCorbusier, Niemeyer or Saarinen may no longer be at the cutting edge of architecture, but Portzamparc gives a new shade and vitality to this tradition.

THE GOOD, THE BAD AND THE SMOOTH

Although architecture requires the help of influential or wealthy patrons, and in France foremost amongst them the government, the country's tradition of protest may make it easier for figures such as Rudy Ricciotti to emerge. A southerner in his accent and origins, Ricciotti makes something of a predictable pattern out of saying surprising things, even openly criticizing colleagues, a rare characteristic in his profession. Though he speaks of rejecting programmatic requirements or breaking molds, Ricciotti is of course obliged in the end to bow to necessity. His tent-like covering for the Visconti Courtyard in the Louvre for the exhibition of Islamic art is meant to avoid turning the space into a "department store," but will it function well within the classical volumes of the royal palace? His National Choreographic Center (Aix-en-Provence, 1999-2005) rises amidst what looks like a charred web of angled beams and columns. In this work, he shows the potential that makes him one of the principal figures to be watched in France. Despite his often controversial statements, Ricciotti is clearly accepted by the "system" in France, as was demonstrated by his selection for the 2006 Grand Prix National for Architecture.

Some more architects selected for this book, in alphabetical order, are Valode & Pistre and Jean-Paul Viguier. These architects have engaged actively in large-scale projects, both within France and in many other countries. The office of Valode & Pistre employs more than 100 staff and demonstrates, much as Jean-Paul Viguier does, a capacity to rationalize and render attractive facilities requiring a high level of performance–corporate offices, hotels, towers, multiplex movie theaters or museums. The technical and esthetic mastery shown by these architects in their separate practices demonstrates the high level to which the art of building has risen in France. Working essentially on privately funded projects, Jean-Paul Viguier, Denis Valode and Jean Pistre are in many ways the epitomy of French rationalists.

Esthetically, French architects probably don't differ greatly from many of their European colleagues, with some exceptions, such as the relative rejection of neo-minimalism or extravagant computer-generated forms. It may well be a certain Cartesian background that makes the French critical of "exaggeration" in architecture, and particularly adept at solving problems in an efficient manner. Without going so far as to confirm clichés, it may be too that a certain spirit of revolt, often visible in the streets of France during political demonstrations, can be discerned in the country's architecture. Rudy Ricciotti demonstrates this tendency as does, in a more gentle and colorful way, Matali Crasset. Needless to say, many other talented French architects could have been chosen for this overview, but the 15 offices presented here do reveal something of the spirit of architecture today in the land of Descartes.

Philip Jodidio

EINLEITUNG

DESCARTES VERZWEIFELT GESUCHT

Kartesianisch? Die Franzosen sagen, sie wären es. René Descartes (1596–1650), Begründer der analytischen Geometrie und des Rationalismus des 17. Jahrhunderts, dürfte für seinen Ausspruch »Cogito ergo sum« (Ich denke, also bin ich) am besten bekannt sein. Ein Überblick über die zeitgenössische französische Architektur verdeutlicht sicherlich ein hohes Maß an gedanklicher Arbeit seitens der Architekten sowie eine Fülle von komplexen Formen, die sich einer einfachen Klassifizierung zu entziehen scheint. Klar ist, dass Trends wie der Minimalismus, der Bauten der englischen Architekten John Pawson oder David Chipperfield kennzeichnet, es schwer hatten, den Ärmelkanal (oder La Manche, wie die Franzosen sagen) zu überqueren. Andererseits sind die Franzosen ganz gewiss auch nicht so in extravagante, computergenerierte Formen verliebt wie ihre holländischen Nachbarn, wenngleich Lars Spuybroek von NOX Architekten sein Maison-Folie in Frankreich bauen konnte (Lille-Wazemmes, 2001). Welches andere Land würde japanische Trendsetterarchitekten für neue Bauten des Centre Pompidou (Shigeru Ban, Metz) oder des Louvre (SANAA, Sejima+Nishizawa, Lens) auswählen? In den vergangenen 25 Jahren hat Frankreich sich an ausländische Architekten gewandt, um von ihnen vielbeachtete Projekte wie die Louvre-Pyramide (I. M. Pei), die Opéra Bastille (Carlos Ott) und den Grande Arche de la Défense (Johann Otto von Spreckelsen) bauen zu lassen. Parallel zur Realisierung dieser großen Projekte (Grand Travaux) wurden in den Mitterrand-Jahren (1981–95) die Talente im eigenen Land entdeckt. Jean Nouvel mit seinem Institut du Monde Arabe an der Seine in Paris, Christian de Portzamparc (Cité de la Musique, Paris) und Dominique Perrault (Bibliothèque Nationale de France) traten aufgrund der beträchtlichen Mittel, die die Regierung für diese neuen Einrichtungen geradezu verschwenderisch zur Verfügung stellte, in die Öffentlichkeit. Fast zeitgleich kam ein anderer Trend auf: Innenarchitekten und Möbeldesigner wie Philippe Starck und Jean-Michel Wilmotte, die eng mit Pei an der Ausstellungsarchitektur des Louvre zusammengearbeitet hatten, erlangten hohe Bekanntheit. Beide Designer haben sich auch mit einigem Erfolg mit architektonischen Projekten befasst. In jüngerer Zeit ist an der Nahtstelle von Design und Architektur eine neue Designergeneration auf der internationalen Bühne aufgetaucht, die oftmals zu Beginn ihrer Karriere in Starcks Büro gearbeitet hat. Patrick Jouin oder Matali Crasset fallen in diese Kategorie. Mit Höhen und Tiefen, die häufig im Zusammenhang mit ökonomischen Überlegungen und unterschiedlich starker staatlicher Einflussnahme stehen, ist es Frankreich gelungen, eine lebendige Architekturkultur am Leben zu erhalten und gleichzeitig – stärker als die meisten anderen hochentwickelten Länder – die Grenzen für Designer aus dem Ausland zu öffnen. Die in diesem Buch gezeigten Architekten wurden auf der Basis neuer Projekte ausgewählt, um einen Überblick über derzeitig vorhandene Stile und technische Möglichkeiten zu geben. Das Alter der Architekten variiert zwischen Anfang 40 (Matali Crasset und Manuelle Gautrand) und Anfang 60 (Jean-Paul Viguier oder Denis Valode), ebenso unterschiedlich sind Größe und Art der Projekte. Christian de Portzamparc, Gewinner des Pritzker-Preis 1994, und Jean Nouvel werden als »Global Player« der internationalen Architekturszene betrachtet, während andere wie etwa Jean-Marie Duthilleul, Chefarchitekt der nationalen französischen Eisenbahn (SNCF), allgemein weniger bekannt sind, obwohl sie einen beträchtlichen Einfluss auf die Öffentlichkeit in Frankreich und im Ausland haben. Kleine Architekturbüros werden großunternehmerisch geführten Teams wie Valode & Pistre gegenübergestellt.

FARBE IST LEBEN

Trotz der Bandbreite der gezeigten Projekte kann es sein, dass sich die rationale, analytische Wesensart, die man mit Descartes in Verbindung bringt, in den Zielen und Methoden der Architekten bemerkbar macht. Matali Crasset, 1965 in Châlon-en-Champagne geboren, studierte an der École Nationale Supérieure de Création Industrielle in Paris und arbeitete anschließend bei Philippe Starck und Thomson Multimedia, bevor sie 1998 ihr eigenes Büro in Paris gründete. »Die Franzosen haben Angst vor Farbe«, behauptet sie, als sie an einem langen Tisch in ihrem Wohn- und Arbeitsatelier im Pariser Stadtteil Belleville sitzt. Wie bei allen ihren Projekten herrscht hier an Blautönen kein Mangel. »Ich glaube wirklich nicht, dass eine fröhliche Umgebung Kindern vorbehalten sein sollte«, sagt sie und unterstützt ihre Aussage mit Projekten wie dem Hi Hotel in Nizza. Crasset versichert: »Farbe ist Leben.« Sie erklärt ihre Ideen als Strömungen und Gefühle; ihr Ansatz ist also weniger utilitaristisch als der vieler traditioneller Architekten. Mit dem Hi Hotel weicht sie am radikalsten von derzeitig geltenden Architektur- und Designvorstellungen ab. Und es scheint, als ob ihre Aufforderung, die Funktionen von Entwürfen neu zu überdenken, gehört wurde. Ob als Lehrende an Designschulen in Kopenhagen, Mailand, Lausanne oder Amsterdam oder durch ihre Teilnahme an der Architekturbiennale 2004 in Peking, für die sie eigens ein Appartement entwarf, oder ihre Teilnahme an einer großen französisch-chinesischen Ausstellung in Shanghai – Crassets Bekanntheit und Einfluss reichen weit über die Grenzen Frankreichs hinaus. Wie ihr Mentor Starck sieht sie ihre Kreativität nicht auf bestimmte Bereiche beschränkt. Sie hat sich aufgemacht, die Grenzen zwischen Design und Architektur neu zu definieren, vielleicht auch aufzuheben. Die Tendenz, die Schranken zwischen Architektur und anderen Disziplinen wie Kunst oder Design niederzureißen, findet sich in vielen Ländern, Crassets Ansatz, geleitet von der Idee einer sanften Rebellion und einer intelligenten Analyse der Mängel moderner Räume, ist jedoch typisch französisch.

Odile Decq, frühere Partnerin des 1998 verstorbenen Benôit Cornette, ist eine andere prominente Frau in der französischen Architekturszene. In jüngerer Zeit fand sie durch ihren von der Topografie inspirierten Entwurf für das Liaunig Museum in Neuhaus, Österreich, internationale Beachtung. Ihr Entwurf für das FRAC Bretagne – Teil einer Reihe von Einrichtungen für zeitgenössische Kunst in Frankreich – verbindet ein spannendes Äußeres mit funktionaler Effizienz. Wie auch Crasset legt Odile Decq nicht nur in architektonischer Hinsicht, sondern auch in ihrer äußeren Erscheinung Wert auf einen erkennbaren Stil. Ihr extravagant gestyltes Haar und ihr Make-up machen sie fraglos zu etwas Besonderem. Sie hat aber auch vielfach bewiesen, dass Frauen, trotz der klaren Männerdominanz, durchaus ihren Platz im französischen Architekturbetrieb finden können.

LERNEN, HOCH ZU FLIEGEN

Punk ist definitiv nicht Jean-Marie Duthilleuls Sache. Duthilleul, Ingenieur und Architekt, schloss sein Studium an der École Polytechnique mit Auszeichnung ab und hat mehr dazu beigetragen, den Schienenverkehr in Frankreich und anderswo neu zu definieren als jeder andere lebende Architekt. Als Chefarchitekt des SNCF war er nicht nur für die Modernisierung solch ehrwürdiger Bahnhöfe wie dem Gare du Nord oder dem Gare Montparnasse in Paris verantwortlich, sondern auch für den Bau einer Reihe neuer Stationen für TGV-Strecken, die von Paris aus nach Norden und Süden führen. In einer etwas zurückhaltenderen Art und Weise als Santiago Calatrava hat Duthilleul den Bahnhof neu erfunden, um ihn zu einem angenehmen Aufenthaltsort zu machen, an dem Licht und hohe Räume die Regel und nicht die Ausnahme sind. Duthilleuls technische Meisterschaft und seine Verbindungen zum mächtigen französischen Eisenbahnmonopol haben es ihm erlaubt, seine Tätigkeit in den letzten Jahren auszuweiten. Mittlerweile arbeitet er in China und in verschiedenen anderen Ländern. Außerdem konnte er diverse andere Projekte realisieren, darunter Bürogebäude und Sakralbauten wie die hier gezeigte Kirche St. François de Molitor in Paris.

Die 1961 geborene Manuelle Gautrand trat in Frankreich in Erscheinung, als sie für die Teilnahme am Wettbewerb für François Pinaults neues Museum für zeitgenössische Kunst ausgewählt wurde. Bemerkenswert daran war, dass es ihr gelang, neben Tadao Ando, Steven Holl, Rem Koolhaas, Dominique Perrault, MVRDV und Álvaro Siza zu bestehen. Neben dem Verwaltungszentrum in Saint-Étienne und der Erweiterung und Instandsetzung des Musée d'Art Moderne in Lille ist ein weiteres Projekt von Gautrand an extrem prominenter Stelle im Bau: 1927 richtete der Autohersteller Citroën einen Showroom mit der Hausnummer 42 auf den Champs Élysées ein. 1931 wurde das Gebäude nach Entwürfen des Architekten von Citroëns Fabrikbauten, Ravazé, sowie des künstlerischen Leiters Pierre Louys umgebaut. Bis 1984 erachtete man den Stil, in dem sie dies taten, als der Automobilmarke angemessen. In der Folge wurde der Showroom als Restaurant genutzt. Da er nicht mehr zeitgemäß war, entschied Citroën 2002, einen internationalen Wettbewerb mit Teilnehmern wie Zaha Hadid, Daniel Libeskind und Christian de Portzamparc zu organisieren. Manuelle Gautrand ging als Siegerin aus dem Wettbewerb hervor. Sie konzipierte den 1200 m² großen Raum komplett neu und entwarf eine komplexe Glassfassade, für die sie das Firmenlogo mit dem umgedrehten doppelten V verwendet und sich so auf subtile Weise auf die alte, so lange bewunderte Art-Deco-Fassade des Showrooms bezieht. Auf einer Abfolge von Podien sollen die erfolgreichen Citroën-Modelle präsentiert werden. Dieses System erlaubt die vollständige Nutzung der beachtlichen Raumhöhe, ohne den Raum zu unterteilen. Mit ihrer Fähigkeit, sich den internationalen »Big Names« in der Architektur zu stellen und komplexe Projekte zu realisieren, hat Gautrand den Weg zu einer subtilen Modernität gewählt, die weder von Vorbildern übernommen noch gänzlich bahnbrechend ist. Sie ist vielleicht das attraktivste Gesicht des französischen Kartesianismus.

Dominique Jakob und Brendan MacFarlane sind kein rein französisches Büro, denn nur Jakob ist Franzose, MacFarlane stammt dagegen aus Neuseeland; die beiden trafen sich in Los Angeles im Büro von Morphosis. Von ihrer anspruchsvollen »blob«-Form für das Restaurant Georges auf dem Centre Pompidou (2000) zu ihrer subtilen und intelligenten Umgestaltung des Appartements des Kunstsammlers Daniel Bosser hat das dynamische Paar seine Fähigkeit unter Beweis gestellt, sich an unterschiedliche Situationen anzupassen und dabei entschieden modern zu bleiben, auch wenn sie im Kontext eines Appartements im Stil von Haussmann oder einer alten Autofabrik arbeiten (Renault International Communication Center, Boulogne, 2005). Mit Gautrand und anderen repräsentieren sie sicherlich die neue Generation französischer Architekten.

DREI ARTEN, DAS SPIEL ZU GEWINNEN

Denjenigen, die sich für aktuelle Architektur interessieren, braucht Jean Nouvel wohl nicht vorgestellt zu werden. Ein Blick auf die Liste seiner in jüngerer Zeit realisierten Projekte sagt eine Menge über seine internationale Bekanntheit aus. Am 16. September 2005 wurde sein phallischer Torre Agbar an der Hauptverkehrsader Avenida Diagonal von Barcelona eingeweiht, zehn Tage später die deutlich kritisierte Erweiterung des Museo Nacional Centro de Arte Reina Sofia in Madrid. Gleichzeitig mit einem 44geschossigen Hochhaus in Katar und einem Appartementhaus in Soho in New York wurde das wichtigste neue Gebäude der letzten Jahren in Frankreich, das Musée du Quai Branly am Quai Branly fertig gestellt. Nur vier Tage nach dessen Eröffnung im Juni wohnte Nouvel der Einweihung des Guthrie Theater in Minneapolis bei. Nouvel lässt die Öffentlichkeit und die Kritiker nicht gleichgültig. Seine Originalität und die Stärke seiner Architektur sind nicht zu bestreiten, ganz bestimmt aber fordert er die gängigen Vorstellungen, wie moderne Architektur auszusehen hat, heraus. Der angehobene, reptilienartige Baukörper des Museums für Kunst und Zivilisation am Quai Branly ist laut seines Entwerfers »anders als alles, was man je in der westlichen Welt gesehen hat«. Bescheidenheit gehört in diesem Fall nicht zu seinen Tugenden, aber Nouvel hat Recht, wenn er die Tatsache betont, dass er mit diesem Gebäude mit so ziemlich allen Konventionen moderner Architektur bricht.

In einem ganz anderen Stil haben es Nouvel mit Shigeru Ban / Jean de Gastines, Anne Lacaton und Jean-Philippe Vassal, Duncan Lewis, Scape Architecture + Block sowie Art'M Architecture in die Hand genommen, eine der bemerkenswerteren Häusergruppe im sozialen Wohnungsbau zu entwerfen. die seit vielen Jahren in Frankreich gebaut wurde. Mit dem Aufstieg zu einem Industriezentrum in der Mitte der 1880er Jahre wurde im Osten der Stadt Mulhouse unter der Leitung der Société mulhousienne des cités ouvrières der Bau einer Arbeitersiedlung mit 200 Wohnhäusern am Stadtrand initiiert. Die durchschnittliche Größe der Häuser von 47 m² betrachtete man damals als großzügig, später wurde sie jedoch zu einem Problem. Pierre Zemp (SOMCO), der sich für den Stadtteil einsetzte, wandte sich im Jahr 2000 an Jean Nouvel und beauftragte ihn mit dem Entwurf neuer Wohnungen in der Tradition der Cité Manifeste (so der Name der Siedlung). Das Baugrundstück, die îlot Schoettlé, liegt am Rand der historischen Cité ouvrière. 2001 brachte Nouvel im Auftrag des Initiators die weiteren Teilnehmer zusammen und die Gesamtbausumme von 6 229 600 Euro für die 60 geplanten Wohnhäuser wurde festgelegt. Der Initiator weist darauf hin, dass trotz der verschiedenen architektonischen Stile – die Häuser von Nouvel und Lacaton & Vassal werden in diesem Buch gezeigt – die Bauten aller beteiligten Architekten dazu tendieren Grenzen aufzuheben, um Öffnungen und einen Übergang zwischen innen und außen zu schaffen, der so wenig deutlich ist, wie es das Klima vor Ort erlaubt. Vielleicht wirkt er etwas harsch, aber mit diesem sozialen Wohnungsbau erreichen Jean Nouvel und die anderen räumliche Qualitäten, Offenheit und eine Güte der Belichtung, die in Frankreich selten sind.

Die Entscheidung der Jury unter Vorsitz von I. M. Pei, Dominique Perraults Entwurf zum Gewinner des Wettbewerbs für das letzte und vielleicht schwierigste Projekt der »Grand Travaux«, die Bibliothèque Nationale de France im 13. Arrondissement von Paris, zu küren, katapultierte Perrault aus relativer Unbekanntheit zum Architektenstar. Ursprünglich als Gruppe von vier geöffneten, 100 Meter hohen Büchern entworfen, wurde die Höhe der Bibliothek in einer intensiv geführten Kontroverse reduziert. Perraults harter, oft in Metallnetze gekleideter Modernismus ist heute so kompromisslos wie 1989, als er mit der Arbeit an der Bibliothek begann. Er betont sein Interesse an moderner Kunst und seine sehr »antimodernistische« Vorliebe, Gebäude in die Erde einzugraben, wie er es mit seinem Velodrom und der Schwimm- und Sprunghalle tat (Berlin, 1992–99). Im Bereich der Kunst ist seine Härte wohl am ehesten mit Richard Serras großmaßstäblichen Corten-Stahlskulpturen zu vergleichen. Perrault riskiert etwas; bisweilen – etwa mit der Bibliothek – bewegt er sich mit seinen Entwürfen absichtlich außerhalb der akzeptierten Norm. Aber korrespondiert das Konzept der Bibliothek mit ihrer Funktion als Ort des Entdeckens und Lesens von Büchern so gut wie es möglich wäre? Revolte ist ein Teil des französischen Charakters und Perrault – und auch Rudy Ricciotti – verkörpern diesen Aspekt der architektonischen Kreativität des Landes.

Christian de Portzamparc ist sowohl durch seine Gebäude als auch durch seine Masterpläne – zum Beispiel für die Avenue de France hinter Perraults Bibliothek – eine einflussreiche Persönlichkeit in der Architekturszene. Als einziger Franzose hat er bislang den Pritzker-Preis gewonnen. Mit Gebäuden wie dem LVMH Tower in der 57th Street in Manhattan oder dem derzeitig im Bau befindlichen Cidade da Música in Rio hat Portzamparc, abgesehen von Nouvel, mehr dafür getan, die Landesfarben ins Ausland zu tragen als jeder andere lebende französische Architekt. Sein Modernismus ist entschieden lyrisch, mit einigen Ausnahmen, zum Beispiel der eher schweren französischen Botschaft am Pariser Platz in Berlin. In Rio wird seine tiefe Bewunderung für Oscar Niemeyers in Beton gegossene Gedankenflüge der Imagination zum Ausdruck kommen. Seine Zeichnungen und Aquarelle machen seinen künstlerischen Hintergrund deutlich, das eigentliche Fundament seiner Architektur ist jedoch seine Gedankenwelt, die es ihm erlaubt, sich einer einfachen Klassifizierung zu entziehen. Der lyrische Modernismus des späten Le Corbusier, Niemeyer oder Saarinen ist wohl nicht mehr der architektonischen Avantgarde zuzurechnen, aber Portzamparc erweitert diese Tradition um eine neue Schattierung und hält sie lebendig.

DER GUTE, DER BÖSE UND DIE GLATTEN
Architektur bedarf der Unterstützung durch einen einflussreichen oder wohlhabenden Förderer – in Frankreich ist dies in der Hauptsache die Regierung.

Aber wohlmöglich erleichtert es die französische Protesttradition Persönlichkeiten wie Rudy Ricciotti in Erscheinung zu treten. Als Südländer mit entsprechendem Aussehen und Akzent macht Ricciotti eine Art vorhersehbare Gewohnheit daraus, überraschende Dinge zu sagen und sogar offen Kollegen zu kritisieren, ein sehr seltenes Verhalten unter Architekten. Obwohl er davon spricht, Anforderungen durch das Raumprogramm zu ignorieren oder aus den vorgefertigten Formen auszubrechen, muss sich natürlich auch Ricciotti letztlich den Notwendigkeiten beugen. Mit der zeltartigen Überdachung des Visconti-Hofes im Louvre, in dem die islamische Kunst ausgestellt werden soll, möchte er vermeiden, den Raum in ein »Kaufhaus« zu verwandeln. Aber wird das »Zelt« in Verbindung mit den klassischen Gebäude des königlichen Palastes auch wirklich funktionieren? Sein Centre Chorégraphique National (Aix-en-Provence, 2000–05) besteht aus etwas, was aussieht wie ein zerrissenes Netz aus geneigten Trägern und Stützen. Mit diesem Projekt zeigt Ricciotti das Potential, das ihn zu einem der Architekten in Frankreich macht, die man im Auge behalten sollte. Trotz seiner oft kontroversen Statements wird Ricciotti eindeutig vom französischen Establishment anerkannt, was seine Auswahl für den Grand Prix National d'Architecture unterstreicht.

Weitere Architekten, die für dieses Buch ausgewählt wurden, sind, in alphabetischer Ordnung, Valode & Pistre und Jean-Paul Viguier. Beide Büros sind an Großprojekten in Frankreich und in vielen anderen Ländern beteiligt. Das Büro von Valode & Pistre hat mehr als 100 Angestellte; es zeigt, ähnlich wie Jean-Paul Viguier, die Fähigkeit zum rationalen Denken und zur Realisierung attraktiver, komplexer Einrichtungen – Büros für Großunternehmen, Hotels, Hochhäuser, Multiplexkinos oder Museen. Die technische und ästhetische Meisterschaft dieser Architekten stellt die hohe Qualität, die die Baukunst in Frankreich erreicht hat, unter Beweis. In vielerlei Hinsicht sind Jean-Paul Viguier, Denis Valode und Jean Pistre, die im Wesentlichen an privatfinanzierte Gebäuden arbeiten, der Inbegriff des französischen Rationalismus.

In ästhetischer Hinsicht unterscheiden sich französische Architekten wahrscheinlich nicht sehr von vielen ihrer europäischen Kollegen. Einige Besonderheiten, wie die relativ deutliche Ablehnung neo-minimalistischer oder extravaganter computergenerierter Formen, sind jedoch festzustellen. Gut möglich, dass ihr kartesianischer Hintergrund zu einer kritischen Haltung gegenüber der architektonischen »Übertreibung« führt, und besonders dafür geeignet ist, Probleme auf effiziente Art und Weise zu lösen. Ohne soweit gehen zu wollen, Klischees zu bestätigen, mag es auch sein, dass ein bestimmter rebellischer Geist, der oftmals politische Demonstrationen auf Frankreichs Straßen begleitet, auch in der Architektur erkennbar ist. Bei Rudy Ricciotti ist diese Tendenz vorhanden, in sanfterer und farbiger Form auch bei Matali Crasset. Es braucht nicht betont zu werden: Viele andere talentierte Architekten hätten für diesen Überblick ausgewählt werden können, aber die hier vorgestellten 15 Büros verraten tatsächlich etwas von dem aktuellen architektonischen Geist in Descartes' Heimat.

Philip Jodidio

INTRODUCTION

RECHERCHE DESCARTES DÉSESPÉRÉMENT

Cartésiens ? Les Français assurent qu'ils le sont. René Descartes (1596–1650) inventa la géométrie analytique et jeta les bases du rationalisme, mais il est sans doute plus connu pour son célèbre « Cogito ergo sum » (je pense donc je suis). Un survol de l'architecture française contemporaine montre à l'évidence une réflexion développée et une richesse de formes complexes qui semblent défier toute classification hâtive. Il est clair, cependant, qu'une tendance comme le minimalisme, illustrée par les architectes anglais John Pawson ou David Chipperfield, a eu beaucoup de difficultés à traverser la Manche. À l'autre extrême, les praticiens français ne sont pas aussi friands des formes extravagantes produites par ordinateur que leurs voisins néerlandais, mais en revanche, c'est en France que Lars Spuybroek, de NOX, a pu construire sa Maison-Folie (Lille-Wazemmes, 2001). Quel autre pays aurait sélectionné des architectes aussi avant-gardistes que Shigeru Ban pour construire les nouvelles installations du Centre Pompidou à Metz, ou SANAA Sejima +Nishizawa, pour l'antenne du Louvre à Lens ? Au cours de ces vingt-cinq dernières années, la France a fait appel à des architectes étrangers pour des projets aussi notables que la Pyramide du Louvre (I. M. Pei), l'Opéra Bastille (Carlos Ott) ou l'Arche de La Défense (Johann Otto von Spreckelsen). Les années Mitterrand (1981–95) firent beaucoup pour révéler les talents nationaux à l'occasion de projets majeurs, les célèbres Grands Travaux. Jean Nouvel, avec l'Institut du Monde arabe au bord de la Seine, Christian de Portzamparc avec la Cité de la Musique, Dominique Perrault et sa Bibliothèque de France se firent connaître du grand public grâce aux substantiels budgets consacrés par les pouvoirs publics à ces ambitieux projets. Une autre tendance émergea dans le même temps, avec l'accès à la notoriété de designers comme Philippe Starck ou Jean-Michel Wilmotte qui travailla étroitement avec Pei sur le projet du Louvre. Ces deux créateurs se sont également intéressés à l'architecture avec un certain succès. Plus récemment, une nouvelle génération de designers, souvent formés au départ par l'agence de Starck, est apparue sur la scène internationale au point de jonction entre le design et l'architecture. Patrick Jouin ou Matali Crasset appartiennent à cette catégorie. Avec des hauts et des bas, souvent liés au contexte économique et au degré des interventions gouvernementales, la France a réussi à maintenir une culture architecturale vivace tout en ouvrant, plus que d'autres pays développés, ses frontières à des intervenants étrangers. Les architectes présentés ici ont été choisis sur leurs travaux récents et dans l'intention de donner une vision d'ensemble des styles et méthodes actuels. Ils se distinguent par leur âge, qui va d'une petite quarantaine (Matali Crasset ou Manuelle Gautrand) aux débuts de la soixantaine (Jean-Paul Viguier ou Denis Valode), mais aussi par l'échelle et la nature de leur travail. Christian de Portzamparc (lauréat du Pritzker Prize en 1994) et Jean Nouvel sont considérés comme des figures majeures de la scène internationale, tandis que d'autres, comme Jean-Marie Duthilleul, architecte en chef de la SNCF, ne sont pas aussi connus du public, même s'ils exercent par leurs œuvres un impact considérable sur la vie quotidienne en France et à l'étranger. La dimension des agences, très variable, va de petites équipes à de grandes structures comme Valode & Pistre.

LA COULEUR C'EST LA VIE

Malgré la variété des travaux présentés ici, il se peut que l'on retrouve un certain caractère analytique, voire rationnel lié à Descartes dans les ambitions et les méthodes de tous ces architectes. Née en 1965 à Châlons-en-Champagne, Matali Crasset a étudié à l'École nationale supérieure de création industrielle à Paris, puis travaillé avec Philippe Starck et chez Thomson Multimédia avant de créer sa propre agence à Paris en 1998. « Les Français ont peur de la couleur », déclare-t-elle, assise derrière une longue table dans sa maison-atelier du quartier de Belleville à Paris. Le lieu n'est d'ailleurs pas plus dénué de touches colorées que son œuvre en général. « Je ne pense vraiment pas que l'on doive réserver aux enfants les environnements chaleureux », dit-elle avec cette assurance que confirment ses réalisations, comme son Hi Hôtel à Nice. Elle affirme que « la couleur c'est la vie » et explique ses idées en termes de courants et de sentiments plutôt que par l'approche utilitariste commune à la plupart des architectes traditionnels, et c'est ce qui semble la distinguer le plus radicalement des normes actuelles de l'architecture et du design. Il semble que son appel à une réévaluation des fonctions du design a été entendu. Que ce soit par l'enseignement du design à Copenhague, Milan, Lausanne et Amsterdam ou à travers ses participations à la récente Biennale d'architecture de Pékin où elle a présenté un appartement ou à une grande exposition franco-chinoise à Shanghai, sa notoriété et son influence ont désormais allègrement franchi les frontières. Comme son ancien mentor Starck, elle n'envisage aucune borne à sa créativité. Elle s'est engagée dans la redéfinition des limites entre design et architecture, voire leur effacement. Ce type de travail sur l'abolition des barrières entre l'architecture et d'autres disciplines comme l'art ou le design progresse dans de nombreux pays, mais Crasset représente une approche spécifiquement française, empreinte d'un esprit de révolte maîtrisée et d'une analyse intelligente de ce qui ne va pas dans l'espace moderne.

Odile Decq est une autre de ces éminentes personnalités féminines de la scène architecturale française. Ancienne associée de Benoît Cornette, disparu en 1998, elle a acquis récemment une reconnaissance internationale grâce à un projet d'inspiration topographique pour le Liaunig Museum à Neuhaus en Autriche. En France, son projet pour le Frac Bretagne, l'un des maillons du réseau public de centres d'art contemporain, conjugue apparence provocante et efficacité fonctionnelle. Comme Crasset, Odile Decq s'est attachée à se créer un style non seulement dans son architecture, mais aussi dans son aspect physique. Certes, ses coiffures et ses maquillages extravagants font qu'on la remarque, mais elle a amplement prouvé par d'autres moyens qu'une femme peut avoir sa place dans le système architectural français, même si la domination masculine y reste toujours aussi nette.

SUR LE SENTIER DE LA GLOIRE

Le look *punk* n'est certainement pas la tasse de thé de Jean-Marie Duthilleul. Brillant diplômé de l'École polytechnique, ingénieur et architecte, il a fait plus pour la redéfinition des transports ferroviaires en France que tout autre architecte vivant. Architecte en chef de la SNCF, il a été en charge non seulement de la modernisation d'installations aussi vénérables que la gare du Nord ou la gare

Montparnasse à Paris, mais également de toute une série de gares nouvelles pour les lignes de TGV vers le sud et le nord de la France. Dans un style un peu moins flamboyant que celui de Santiago Calatrava, il a réussi à faire de la gare ferroviaire un lieu plus agréable, où la lumière et les vastes espaces sont la règle plutôt que l'exception. Sa maîtrise technique et ses liens avec le puissant monopole des chemins de fer français lui ont permis de se diversifier au cours de ces dernières années ; il a ainsi travaillé en Chine et dans plusieurs autres pays. Il a également réalisé un certain nombre d'autres projets, notamment des immeubles de bureaux et des édifices religieux, comme l'église publiée ici.

Manuelle Gautrand, née en 1961, a brusquement accédé à la notoriété en France lorsqu'elle a été retenue dans la sélection d'architectes appelés à participer au concours organisé par François Pinault pour son musée d'art contemporain. Le plus remarquable est que sa proposition fit bonne figure face à Tadao Ando, Steven Holl, Rem Koolhaas, Dominique Perrault, MVRDV et Álvaro Siza. En dehors de ses chantiers pour le Centre administratif de Saint-Étienne et pour l'extension et la rénovation du musée d'Art moderne Lille Métropole, elle s'est lancée dans des projets de haute visibilité à Paris. Le constructeur automobile Citroën avait installé ses salons d'exposition sur les Champs-Élysées en 1927. Le designer de l'entreprise, Maurice-Jacques Ravazé, et son directeur artistique, Pierre Louÿs, furent chargés en 1931 de transformer l'immeuble dans un style qui fut conservé jusqu'en 1984, puis modernisé. Mais ce show-room qui abritait aussi un restaurant était devenu vraiment démodé lorsque Citroën décida, en 2002, d'organiser un concours international auquel participèrent Zaha Hadid, Daniel Libeskind et Christian de Portzamparc. Ce fut Manuelle Gautrand qui le remporta et fut chargée de reconstruire entièrement cet immeuble de 1200 m². À partir du motif du chevron, emblème de la firme, elle a conçu une façade complexe en verre qui laisse voir les divers plateaux sur lesquels les véhicules seront présentés et elle a conservé une référence discrète à l'ancienne façade Art Déco, si longtemps admirée. Le système de plates-formes prévu permet d'utiliser pleinement la hauteur considérable de cet immeuble très étroit sans en rompre le volume. Dans sa capacité à se mesurer aux « poids-lourds » de l'architecture internationale et à entreprendre des projets complexes, Manuelle Gautrand a su évoluer vers une modernité subtile, qui n'est ni banale ni révolutionnaire. Elle est peut-être le visage le plus séduisant du cartésianisme français.

Dominique Jakob et Brendan MacFarlane ne sont certainement pas l'agence française la plus typique de ce groupe. Dominique Jakob est française mais Brendan MacFarlane est né en Nouvelle-Zélande et le couple s'est connu chez Morphosis à Los Angeles. De ses *blobs* sophistiqués pour le restaurant Georges au Centre Pompidou (2000) à sa transformation subtile et intelligente de l'appartement du collectionneur d'art Daniel Bosser, ce couple dynamique a montré une grande capacité à s'adapter à des situations très diverses et à rester résolument moderne, que ce soit dans le cadre d'un appartement post-haussmannien ou dans celui d'une ancienne usine d'automobiles (Centre de communication international Renault, Boulogne-Billancourt, 2005). Avec d'autres praticiens, telle Manuelle Gautrand, Jakob +MacFarlane constituent la relève de l'architecture française.

TROIS VOIES ROYALES

Jean Nouvel n'est certainement plus à présenter aux amateurs d'architecture contemporaine. Un coup d'œil sur la liste de ses derniers projets témoigne de sa notoriété internationale. Sa tour phallique Agbar en bordure du grand axe de Barcelone, l'Avenida Diagonal, a été inaugurée le 16 septembre 2005. Dix jours plus tard, c'était son extension du centre d'Art contemporain Reina Sofia à Madrid, cette fois accompagnée de critiques senties. Tout en achevant une tour de quarante-quatre étages au Qatar et un immeuble d'habitations à SoHo (New York), il vient de signer le plus intéressant sans doute des nouveaux bâtiments institutionnels érigés en France depuis longtemps, le musée du quai Branly à Paris. Quatre jours après son inauguration en juin 2006, il se trouvait déjà à Minneapolis pour l'inauguration du Guthrie Theater. Nouvel ne laisse indifférents ni les critiques ni le public. Son originalité et la force de son architecture sont indéniables et il remet en jeu les perceptions de ce à quoi l'architecture moderne est supposée ressembler. Le volume reptilien surélevé du musée du quai Branly est, selon son auteur, « différent de tout ce que l'on a pu voir en Occident ». Si la modestie n'est pas sa qualité première, Nouvel a raison de souligner qu'il est ici en rupture avec la plupart des conventions de l'architecture contemporaine.

Dans un style totalement différent, Nouvel, Shigeru Ban/Jean de Gastines, Anne Lacaton et Jean-Philippe Vassal, Duncan Lewis, Scape Architecture + Block et Art'M Architecture ont entrepris de concevoir l'un des plus remarquables ensembles de logements sociaux vus en France depuis longtemps. Ville alsacienne devenue centre industriel au milieu des années 1880, Mulhouse avait créé à l'orée de sa banlieue un quartier de logements ouvriers composé de deux cents maisons, sous la houlette de la Société mulhousienne des cités ouvrières. La taille moyenne de ces logements était de 47 m², ce qui paraissait généreux à l'époque mais finit par poser problème. Un promoteur, Pierre Zemp (directeur de la Somco) contacta Jean Nouvel en 2000 pour lui demander de travailler sur un projet inspiré de la tradition de cette « Cité Manifeste », puisque tel était son nom. Le site retenu, l'îlot Schoettlé, est contigu à la cité ouvrière. Nouvel réunit plusieurs de ses confrères en 2001 et un budget global de construction de 6 300 000 € fut alloué pour les soixante logements prévus. Comme le souligne le promoteur, malgré les différences de styles des architectes consultés (les projets de Nouvel et de Lacaton & Vassal sont publiés dans cet ouvrage), tous s'efforcent de rendre les limites moins précises, de créer des ouvertures et des transitions entre l'intérieur et l'extérieur, autant que le permet le climat local. Malgré leur aspect un peu rude, ces logements sociaux répondent, grâce à Jean Nouvel et aux autres architectes intervenants, à des critères d'espace, de lumière et de qualité rarement atteints en France.

Dominique Perrault a jailli d'une relative obscurité lorsqu'un jury présidé par I. M. Pei l'a choisi pour prendre en charge le dernier et peut-être le plus difficile des Grands Travaux, la Bibliothèque nationale de France dans le XIIIᵉ arrondissement de Paris. Conçue au départ comme un ensemble de quatre livres ouverts de cent mètres de haut chacun, sa hauteur a dû être revue à la baisse suite à une intense controverse. Le modernisme brut des créations de Perrault, souvent revêtues de résilles métalliques, reste aussi rigide aujourd'hui qu'il l'était en 1989 quand il commença à travailler sur la Bibliothèque. Mettant en avant son intérêt pour l'art contemporain, il a adopté la tendance « anti-moderne » qui consiste à « enterrer » ses bâtiments, par exemple le vélodrome olympique et la piscine de Berlin (1992–99). La famille artistique dont ses réalisations se rapprochent le plus est sans doute celle des énormes sculptures en acier Corten de Richard Serra. Perrault prend des risques, concevant parfois volontairement hors normes, comme dans le cas de la Bibliothèque. Mais ses plans sont-ils vraiment bien adaptés à la fonction de conserver et de lire des livres ? L'esprit de révolte fait partie de la personnalité française et Perrault, comme Rudy Ricciotti, incarne cet aspect de la créativité architecturale nationale.

Christian de Portzamparc, dont l'influence est manifeste, que ce soit à travers ses constructions ou ses plans d'urbanisme, comme celui pour l'avenue de France derrière la Bibliothèque de Perrault, est le seul Français titulaire du Pritzker Prize. Avec des réalisations comme la tour LVMH sur la 57e Rue à Manhattan ou le Centre de la musique qu'il construit actuellement à Rio de Janeiro, il a fait plus pour défendre les couleurs de son pays à l'étranger que pratiquement tout autre architecte français vivant, à part Nouvel. Son modernisme est incontestablement lyrique, hormis quelques exceptions, telle la massive ambassade de France sur la Pariser Platz à Berlin. À Rio il montrera son admiration profonde pour les envolées de béton à la Niemeyer. Ses dessins et aquarelles révèlent la dimension artistique de son travail, mais son architecture trouve ses racines profondes dans une réflexion personnelle qui le fait échapper à toute classification. Le modernisme lyrique de Le Corbusier, de Niemeyer ou de Saarinen n'est peut-être plus à l'avant-garde de l'architecture, mais Portzamparc a donné une vitalité nouvelle à cette tradition.

DE L'EXTRÊME AU JUSTE MILIEU

Bien que l'architecture nécessite l'aide de commanditaires puissants ou riches, et en France proches du pouvoir, la tradition protestataire de ce pays a facilité l'émergence de figures comme Rudy Ricciotti. Homme du Sud, comme son accent l'indique, Ricciotti aime provoquer, surprendre, et il n'hésite pas à critiquer ouvertement ses confrères, chose peu courante dans cette profession. Bien qu'il parle souvent de rejeter les contraintes des programmes ou de « casser les moules », il sait aussi se plier aux nécessités. Sa couverture en forme de tente pour la cour Visconti du Louvre, destinée à abriter les collections d'art islamique, entend éviter de transformer cet espace en « grand magasin ». Mais ne sera-t-elle pas un peu incongrue au sein des volumes classiques de ce palais royal ? Son Centre national de la chorégraphie (Aix-en-Provence, 2000–05) semble s'élever au milieu de ce qui ressemble à un enchevêtrement de poutres et de poteaux tordus et carbonisés. Dans ce projet, il témoigne du potentiel qui fait de lui l'une des principales figures à suivre en France. Malgré ses déclarations souvent controversées, il a aujourd'hui été accepté par le « système », comme le montre l'attribution du Grand Prix national d'architecture 2006.

Des autres architectes sélectionnés pour cet ouvrage sont, par ordre alphabétique, Valode & Pistre et Jean-Paul Viguier. Ils sont largement engagés dans des projets à grande échelle, aussi bien en France qu'à l'étranger. L'agence de Va-

lode & Pistre emploie plus de cent personnes et fait preuve, comme celle de Viguier, d'un vrai talent pour rationaliser et rendre attractifs des équipements qui demandent de hauts niveaux de performance : bureaux, hôtels, tours, cinémas multiplex ou musées. La maîtrise esthétique et technique de ces architectes est une illustration du niveau de qualité atteint par l'architecture contemporaine française. Travaillant essentiellement pour des projets privés, Jean-Paul Viguier, Denis Valode et Jean Pistre sont l'illustration par excellence du rationalisme français.

Esthétiquement, les architectes français ne diffèrent sans doute pas beaucoup de leurs confrères européens, mais ils présentent certains particularismes, comme le relatif rejet du néo-minimalisme ou des formes extravagantes issues de la création numérique. Il se peut même que ce soit ce fond de cartésianisme qui rende les Français si critiques à l'égard de « l'exagération » en architecture et particulièrement férus dans la recherche de solutions efficaces. Sans aller jusqu'à confirmer certains clichés, il est également possible qu'un certain esprit de révolte, souvent visible dans les manifestations politiques locales, puisse infiltrer l'architecture. Rudy Ricciotti témoigne de cette tendance de même que, sur un mode plus doux et coloré, Matali Crasset. Inutile de dire que beaucoup d'autres architectes français de talent pourraient figurer dans ce florilège, mais les quinze agences présentées ici sont caractéristiques de l'esprit de l'architecture d'aujourd'hui au pays de Descartes.

Philip Jodidio

1

MATALI CRASSET

MATALI CRASSET
26, rue du Buisson Saint Louis
75010 Paris

Tel: +33 1 42 40 99 89
Fax: +33 1 42 40 99 98
e-mail: matali.crasset@wanadoo.fr
Web: www.matalicrasset.com

Born in 1965 in Châlon-en-Champage, **MATALI CRASSET** studied at the École Nationale Supérieure de Création Industrielle in Paris. She received her diploma in 1991 and left for Milan, where she worked as a designer. She returned to Paris to work with Philippe Starck and Thomson Multimedia before creating her own office in 1998. Matali Crasset has designed furniture and domestic objects, as well as exhibitions and interiors. Her exhibition work includes the "Paris-Milano" and "Bulb" shows for the design magazine *Intramuros*, as well as the "Tendence" fair in Frankfurt (2000), Archilab in Orléans (2001) and several projects for Hermès. She has also created installations that call into question architectural space ("Casaderme," 2002). Her work as an interior architect includes the Red Cell advertising agency Paris (2001); her own studio-house, Paris (2001); a private house near Lake Annecy (2001); the Hi-Hotel, Nice (2003); the BHV store, Belle-Épine (2005); the SM museum of contemporary art, s'Hertogenbosch, The Netherlands (2005); Vegetable, an ephemeral restaurant, Paris (2005); the Lieu Commun store, Paris (2005); and the Vert Anis restaurant, Annecy (2005). Her current work includes a residence in Tarifa, Spain, and the Sleg House in Nice. Since 2006, Matali Crasset has been in charge of a new design concept for the Formule 1 chain of hotels.

HI HOTEL
NICE
2001·03

FLOOR AREA: 3000 m²
CLIENT: HCF SARL
COST: not disclosed

Matali Crasset's Hi Hotel in Nice opened in March 2003. Located near the shore of the Mediterranean and the Promenade des Anglais, the main seaside thoroughfare of Nice, the hotel was created in collaboration with the entrepreneurs Philippe Chapelet and Patrick Elouarghi in a 1930s building that had once been a boarding house. The hotel's 38 rooms are of nine different types, created expressly to challenge assumptions about design and the use of space. In theory, guests' rooms are selected according to a questionnaire they are asked to fill out–matching designs with personalities. A table becomes a bed and a bed a bathtub as Crasset makes an emphatic leap towards alternative forms of interior organization. As it is in her work in general, color is a constant concern—even when Matali Crasset eradicates it in the "White Room." The "Happy Bar," located at the center of the hotel, bathes visitors in her typical saturated colors and video imagery produced, in part, by her office. In a related initiative, Crasset created Hometrack, a system intended to permit viewers to program their own contemporary art favorites on television with a digital telephone connection. Though very much in the spirit of her other work, the Hi Hotel is Matali Crasset's first full-fledged attempt at a "total design" project, where she controls everything, from the graphics, to the furniture and the interior architecture. The white porcelain dinner service called "Link," which she designed for Hi, was made by the Manufacture de Porcelaine de Monaco. The dinner service has four containers, with the bowl intended to be used as a cup, a teacup as a soup bowl and so on. The designer goes so far as to include eating manners in her design concept. F Communications, a French electronic music label, created the sound environment for the hotel under her supervision.

Das Hi Hotel in Nizza von Matali Crasset in der Nähe des Mittelmeers und der großen Uferstraße Promenade des Anglais wurde im März 2003 eröffnet. Das Projekt wurde in Zusammenarbeit mit den Unternehmern Philippe Chapelet und Patrick Elouarghi realisiert und in eine ehemalige Pension aus den 1930er Jahren integriert. Es hat 38 Zimmer in neun verschiedenen Ausstattungen, die bewusst herkömmliche Vorstellungen von Design und der Nutzung von Raum herausfordern. Die Zimmer werden – theoretisch – nach einem von den Gästen auszufüllenden Frageformular ausgewählt, um den zum jeweiligen Design passenden Gast herauszufinden. Ein Tisch wird zum Bett, ein Bett zur Badewanne – Crasset macht einen entschiedenen Schritt zu alternativen Formen der Innenraumgestaltung. Wie bei allen ihren Projekten spielt Farbe eine wichtige Rolle – auch dann, wenn sie eliminiert wird, wie im »Chambre Blanche«. In der »Happy Bar« im Zentrum des Hotels taucht der Besucher in die für Crasset typischen satten Farben und eine Videobilderwelt ein, die z. T. in ihrem Büro generiert wurde. Bei »Hometrack«, einem ähnlichen Projekt der Architektin, kann der Fernsehzuschauer seine Favoriten der zeitgenössischen Kunst über eine digitale Telefonleitung in sein TV-Gerät einprogrammieren. Das Hi Hotel steht in einer Reihe mit anderen Projekten Crassets, ist aber der erste ausgereifte Versuch eines ganzheitlichen Designs, bei dem sie alles, von der Grafik über die Möblierung bis zur Innenarchitektur, kontrollierte. Das für das Hi Hotel entworfene Tafelgeschirr »Link« aus weißem Porzellan wurde in der Manufacture de Porcelaine de Monaco angefertigt. Es umfasst vier Gefäße, von denen die Schüssel auch als Tasse benutzt werden kann, eine Teetasse als Suppentasse usw.; die Designerin integriert also sogar Essgewohnheiten in ihr Designkonzept. Unter Crassets Leitung entwarf F Communications, ein französisches Label für elektronische Musik, die akustische Ausstattung des Hotels.

Cet hôtel signé Matali Crasset a ouvert ses portes en mars 2003. Situé près de la Promenade des Anglais à Nice, il a été créé en collaboration avec ses promoteurs, Philippe Chapelet et Patrick Elouarghi, dans un ancien pensionnat des années 1930. Les trente-huit chambres, de neuf types différents, sont autant d'occasions de remettre en question les idées reçues sur le design et l'utilisation de l'espace. En théorie, la chambre est accordée au voyageur en fonction d'un questionnaire qu'il doit remplir afin que le décor corresponde à sa personnalité. Matali Crasset a radicalement choisi des formes alternatives d'organisation intérieure : la table se transforme en lit, le lit en baignoire, etc. Comme toujours chez elle, la couleur est un souci constant, même lorsqu'elle l'élimine complètement comme dans sa « Chambre blanche ». Le « Happy Bar », au centre de l'hôtel, plonge le visiteur dans une saturation de couleurs et d'images vidéo produites en partie par son agence. Sur la même lancée, Crasset a créé « Hometrack », un système qui permet aux spectateurs de programmer leurs œuvres d'art contemporain favorites sur une télévision numérique. Bien que parfaitement dans l'esprit de ses autres réalisations, le Hi Hotel est la première tentative de grande envergure de la designer de s'attaquer à un projet de *total design* dans lequel elle contrôle tout, du graphisme au mobilier en passant par l'architecture intérieure. Le service de porcelaine « Link » qu'elle a spécialement dessiné pour l'hôtel a été réalisé par la Manufacture de porcelaine de Monaco. Il se compose de quatre récipients et d'une coupe qui peut faire office de tasse à café ou à thé, de bol à soupe, etc. : même les façons de manger font maintenant partie du concept. F Communications, un label français de musique électronique, a créé l'environnement sonore de l'hôtel, sous la supervision de M. Crasset.

Above, the lobby and Internet space with "Interface" armchairs designed for the Hi Hotel and edited by Domodinamica. Left, the "Happy Bar" which has a resident DJ and shows videos—here "Peut-être un DVD" by Olivier Bardin. Right, the Happy Bar.

Lobby und Internetbereich mit den für das Hi Hotel entworfenen »Interface« - Sesseln, die von Domodinamica produziert wurden. Links: Die »Happy Bar« mit hauseigenem DJ und Videos, die gezeigt werden – hier »Peut-être un DVD« von Olivier Bardin. Rechts: Die »Happy Bar«.

Le hall de réception et l'espace Internet. Les fauteuils « Interface » conçus pour le Hi Hotel sont édités par Domodinamica. À gauche, le « Happy Bar » à DJ résident et projections vidéo ; on voit ici celle d'Olivier Bardin » Peut-être un DVD ». À droite, le « Happy Bar ».

Upper left, "Digital"–one of the nine room concepts created by Matali Crasset. Upper right, and lower left, "White & White", another of the room concepts, where bed and table are one and the same. Lower right, "Rendez-vous," a concept featuring the Hi.stone lava bathtub and "Il capriccio di Ugo" armchair.

»Digital« – eines der neun von Matali Crasset entworfenen Konzepte für die Hotelzimmer. Oben rechts und unten links: In »White & White« bilden Bett und Tisch eine Einheit. Unten rechts: »Rendez-vous«, mit einer Wanne aus Lavastein und dem Sessel »Il capriccio di Ugo«.

« Digital » – l'une des neuf chambres concepts créées par Matali Crasset. En haut à droite et en bas à gauche, « White & White », autre chambre dans laquelle le lit et la table ne font qu'un. En bas à droite, la chambre « Rendez-vous », dotée d'une baignoire en lave « Hi.stone » et du fauteuil « Il capriccio di Ugo. »

"Indoor Terrace," another room concept in which the furniture is concentrated in the center of the room. The bathroom is lit from the interior and serves as a kind of lantern.

Auch beim Zimmerkonzept »Indoor Terrace« konzentriert sich die Möblierung in der Mitte des Raumes. Das Bad wird von innen beleuchtet und bildet eine Art Laterne.

« Indoor Terrace », autre chambre concept dans laquelle le mobilier est concentré au milieu de la pièce. La salle de bains éclairée de l'intérieur fait office de « veilleuse ».

Another of the room concepts, called "Strate," converts the usual horizontal organization of space to the vertical, "to change the visitor's everyday point of view."

Beim Zimmerkonzept »Strate« wird die übliche horizontale Raumgliederung durch eine vertikale ersetzt, »um die Alltagsperspektive der Gäste zu verändern«.

La chambre « Strate » fait basculer l'organisation habituelle de l'espace de l'horizontale à la verticale, « pour changer le point de vue quotidien du visiteur ».

TOUT'OUVERT
NICE
2005

FLOOR AREA: 40 m²
CLIENT: Carole Heleine, Tout'ouvert
COST: not disclosed

It was as a result of seeing the Hi Hotel that Carole Heleine decided to sell her apartment in Nice and to ask Matali Crasset to redesign her canine coiffure shop to make it a place to live and work. The idea of creating a multipurpose space in such close quarters (40 m²) appealed to Matali Crasset and she happily accepted the challenge. She used her own furniture, such as the "Hi Pouf" or the "Hi Light" (Domodinamica). The working space is visible from the street, giving the owner a closer connection to the public. With her usual affection for bright colors, Crasset has deliberately contrasted the shop front with the surrounding stores—Tout'ouvert is open, dynamic and fresh, as she says. The shop's name is in fact a play on words in French since the term "toutou" signifies "dog" while the full name "Tout'ouvert" means "completely open." The interior is built around a metal and glass structure that supports the mezzanine, and a long acid-green resin-stratified band runs through the space "like a garden hedge," affording the client some intimacy despite the very small floor area. As Matali Crasset says, "acid green is associated with sky blue to amplify the volumes and allow them to breathe." One step down from the canine coiffure space, the private area includes a kitchen with a bar top. A space for two beds, a fuchsia-colored dressing room and a "comfort area" with violet and fuchsia poufs complete the design.

Nachdem Carole Heleine das Hi Hotel gesehen hatte, beschloss sie, ihr Appartement in Nizza zu verkaufen und Matali Crasset damit zu beauftragen, ihren Hundesalon in einen gemeinsamen Lebens- und Arbeitsraum umzugestalten. Die Idee, einen multifunktionalen Raum auf einer nur 40 m² großen Fläche zu schaffen, reizte Matali Crasset, und sie nahm die Herausforderung gerne an. Bei dem Projekt kamen ihre eigenen Möbelentwürfe zum Einsatz, z. B. »Hi Pouf« und »Hi Light« (Domodinamica). Der Arbeitsbereich ist von der Straße aus einsehbar und schafft so eine größere Nähe zwischen Inhaberin und Öffentlichkeit. Mit ihrer Liebe zu leuchtenden Farben hat Crasset den Salon bewusst in Kontrast zu den Läden in der Umgebung gesetzt – Tout'ouvert ist nach ihrer Aussage offen, dynamisch und frisch. Der Name des Salons ist ein Wortspiel aus dem französischen »toutou« für »Wauwau« und »ouvert« für »offen«. Der Innenraum entwickelt sich um einen Einbau aus Metall und Glas, der das Zwischengeschoss trägt, und ein langes kunstharzverstärktes quietschgrünes Regal, das den Raum »wie eine Hecke« durchschneidet und der Bauherrin trotz der sehr geringen Grundfläche etwas Privatsphäre bietet. Nach Matali Crasset »werden die Farben Quietschgrün und Himmelblau eingesetzt, um das Raumvolumen zu vergrößern und ihm das Atmen zu erlauben«. Der private Bereich mit einer auch als Bar fungierenden Küche liegt eine Stufe niedriger als der Bereich des Hundesalons. Zwei Betten, ein fuchsiafarbener Ankleideraum und eine »Komfortzone« mit violetten und fuchsiafarbenen Puffs vervollständigen den Raum.

C'est après avoir visité le Hi Hotel que Carole Heleine a décidé de vendre son appartement niçois et de demander à Matali Crasset de transformer sa boutique de soins canins en lieu de vie et de travail. L'idée de créer un espace multifonctions sur une surface aussi petite (40 m²) a séduit la designer qui a volontiers accepté de relever ce défi. Elle a utilisé ses propres meubles, comme le Hi Pouf et la Hi Light (Domodinamica). L'espace de travail, visible depuis la rue, est en lien direct avec l'animation de celle-ci. Toujours adepte des couleurs vives, M. Crasset a choisi de faire contraster la façade de la boutique avec celles des magasins voisins. « Tout'ouvert » – bien sûr un jeu de mot à partir de toutou et d'ouvert... – est ouvert, dynamique et frais, selon ses propres termes. L'intérieur s'organise autour d'une structure en verre et en métal qui soutient une mezzanine, et un long bandeau de résine stratifiée vert acide qui court autour du volume comme « une haie de jardin », offre à la clientèle une certaine intimité malgré la petitesse des lieux. Comme le précise Matali Crasset, « le vert acide est associé au ciel bleu, il amplifie les volumes et leur permet de respirer ». Une marche plus bas que l'« espace toutou » commence la zone privée qui comprend une cuisine avec bar. Un espace pour deux lits, un dressing-room fuchsia et une « aire de confort » à poufs violets et fuchsia complètent le dispositif.

tout'ouvert

The actual dog salon, a detail of the bathroom, the Tout'ouvert logo that shows the plan of the space, and a view of the waiting area. This page, the open kitchen and the ladder leading to the rooms. Right, the façade of the shop at night.

Der eigentliche Hundesalon, ein Badezimmerdetail, Logo von Tout'ouvert mit dem abstrahierten Grundriss des Salons, Blick in den Wartebereich. Diese Seite: Die offene Küche und die Leiter, die zu den Räumen führt. Rechts: Nachtansicht des Salons.

En haut, l'espace de toilettage pour chiens, un détail de la salle de bains, le logo Tout'ouvert (qui est en fait le plan du lieu) et une vue de la « salle d'attente ». Sur cette page, la cuisine ouverte et l'échelle conduisant à la chambre en mezzanine. À droite, la façade de la boutique vue de nuit.

ODILE DECQ

2

ODILE DECQ BENOÎT CORNETTE
Architectes Urbanistes
11, rue des Arquebusiers
75003 Paris

Tel: +33 1 42 71 27 41
Fax: +33 1 42 71 27 42
e-mail: odbc@odbc-paris.com
Web: www.odbc-paris.com

ODILE DECQ was born in 1955 in Laval and obtained her degree in architecture (DPLG) at the University of Paris (UPG) in 1978. She studied urbanism at the Institut d'Études Politiques in Paris (1979) and founded her office in 1980. Her former partner, Benoît Cornette, died in 1998. She has designed a number of apartment buildings in Paris (1988, 1995, 1997 and currently); three buildings for Nantes University (1993–99); the French Pavilion at the 1996 Architecture Biennale in Venice; and the Shiatzy Chen fashion boutique on the rue Saint Honoré in Paris. She has worked recently on a refurbishment of the UNESCO Conference Hall, Paris (2001); a renovation of the Cureghem Veterinary School, Brussels (2001); the Assindustria office building in Terni, Italy (2003) and the Liaunig Museum in Neuhaus, Austria (2004). She is currently building the FRAC Bretagne; a residential and commercial building in Florence; and a new villa in Ninjing, China. The winner of the Golden Lion at the Venice Architecture Biennale (1996) and the 1999 Benedictus Award for the Faculty of Economics and the Law Library at the University of Nantes, she has taught at the École Spéciale d'Architecture in Paris since 1992, and has been a guest professor at the Technische Hochschule,Vienna (1998), the Bartlett School of Architecture, London (1998–2000) and Columbia University in New York (2001 and 2003).

FRAC BRETAGNE
RENNES
2005 -

FLOOR AREA: 5000 m^2
CLIENT: Brittany Region
COST: €5.2 million

The winner of a competition organized by the regional authority of Brittany, this project includes exhibition and storage space, a library, offices, a conference room and a café. The FRAC (Fonds regional d'art contemporain or Regional Fund for Contemporary Art) is part of a web of contemporary art institutions created in France in the 1980s by the Minister of Culture, Jack Lang. As Odile Decq says, her project "reinterprets the dual and apparently contradictory ideas of the insertion of a building into an urban context and immaterial escape, of the natural and the artificial, of the heavy and the light and of shadow and light." For the exterior she has employed black architectural concrete for the northern volume and black-blue stainless steel and gray, semi-reflective glass for the southern part of the structure. Within, where an atrium and ramps offer access to public spaces, a lighter color of concrete is used in the north, while stainless steel and red lacquer dominate in the south. Polished concrete is used on most of the floors with the exception of the Resource Center and offices, where colored resin is employed. The exhibition galleries have white walls and ceilings, "for reasons of flexibility," and are described as "neutral but not necessarily rectangular." Decq insists that the entrance area, foyer, ramps and passages, as well as an upper terrace, are intended to encourage the visitor to explore the entire building.

Der Entwurf ging als Gewinner aus einem von der regionalen Verwaltung der Bretagne ausgelobten Wettbewerb hervor und umfasst den Ausstellungsbereich, Lagerflächen, Bibliothek, Büros, einen Konferenzraum und ein Café. Das FRAC Bretagne ist Teil eines Netzwerks von Einrichtungen für zeitgenössische Kunst, das in den 1980er Jahren durch den damaligen Kulturminister Jack Lang gegründet wurde. Die Abkürzung FRAC steht für »Fonds Régional d'Art Contemporain« oder »Regionalfonds für zeitgenössische Kunst«. Nach Odile Decq interpretiert der Entwurf duale und scheinbar widersprüchliche Vorstellungen neu: Er ist zugleich architektonischer Bestandteil in einem städtischen Kontext und geistiger Fluchtort; natürlich und künstlich, schwer und leicht, Licht und Schatten«. Als Fassadenmaterial wählte die Architektin schwarzen Sichtbeton für den nördlichen Teil des Gebäudes und schwarzblauen Edelstahl sowie graues, teilreflektierendes Glas für den südlichen Teil. Die öffentlichen Räume werden über ein Atrium und Rampen erschlossen. In diesem Bereich wird im Norden ein hellerer Beton verwendet, während im Süden Edelstahl und roter Lack dominieren. Mit Ausnahme des Ressourcenzentrums und der Büros, die Böden aus eingefärbtem Kunstharz haben, bestehen die meisten anderen Böden aus geschliffenem Beton. »Aus Gründen der Flexibilität« sind die Wände und Decken in den Ausstellungsbereichen weiß gehalten; sie werden als »neutral, aber nicht unbedingt rechtwinklig« beschrieben. Eingangsbereich, Foyer, Rampen und Verbindungen sowie die obere Terrasse sollen zu einem Besuch des gesamten Gebäudes animieren.

Gagnant d'un concours organisé par la Région Bretagne, ce projet comprend un espace d'exposition, des réserves, une bibliothèque, des bureaux, une salle de conférences et un café. Ce Frac (Fonds régional d'art contemporain) fait partie du réseau d'institutions consacrées à l'art contemporain mis en place dans les années 1980 par Jack Lang, alors ministre de la Culture. Pour Odile Decq, « ce projet réinterprète ces idées duales et apparemment contradictoires que sont l'insertion d'un bâtiment dans un contexte urbain et l'espace immatériel, le naturel et l'artificiel, le lourd et le léger, l'ombre et la lumière ». Pour l'extérieur, elle a choisi un béton architectural noir pour la partie nord, de l'acier inoxydable bleu noir et du verre semi-réfléchissant gris pour la partie sud. À l'intérieur, où un atrium et des rampes permettent l'accès du public, un béton de couleur plus claire recouvre la plupart des sols , sauf ceux du Centre de ressources et des bureaux, qui utilisent une résine colorée. Les galeries d'exposition aux murs et plafonds blancs « pour des raisons de souplesse » sont décrites comme « neutres mais pas forcément rectangulaires ». L'entrée, le hall d'accueil, les rampes et des passages ainsi que la terrasse supérieure sont pensés pour inciter le visiteur à parcourir le bâtiment dans sa totalité.

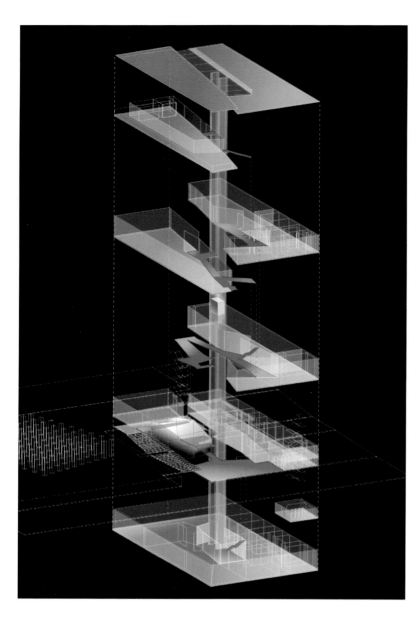

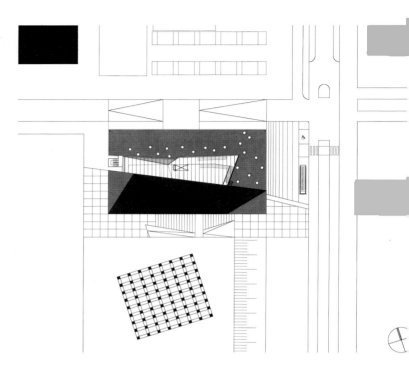

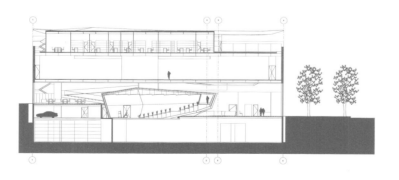

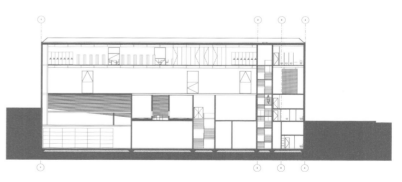

Despite the dynamic appearance of the computer perspectives of this building, sections and plans show that the design of the structure is largely rectilinear and easily comprehensible.

Auf den Computerperspektiven wirkt das Gebäude sehr dynamisch. Schnitte und Grundrisse zeigen jedoch einen im Wesentlichen rechtwinkligen und leicht lesbaren Entwurf.

Malgré l'aspect dynamique des perspectives élaborées par ordinateur, les plans et les coupes montrent que la construction est plutôt rectiligne et assez simple.

Although computer perspectives undoubtedly give the impression that the building will be even lighter than it could be in reality, the fact remains that Decq is approaching an active synthesis of contemporary design and good "old-fashioned" modern efficiency.

Auch wenn die Computerperspektiven das Gebäude noch leichter zeigen, als es in der Realität sein wird, wird deutlich, dass Decq sich einer Synthese aus zeitgenössischem Design und »altmodischer« moderner Effizienz annähert.

Si les perspectives de synthèse donnent l'impression que le bâtiment est plus léger qu'il ne peut l'être en réalité, on constate sur le terrain qu'Odile Decq conjugue les techniques de conception contemporaines et une efficacité moderne « à l'ancienne ».

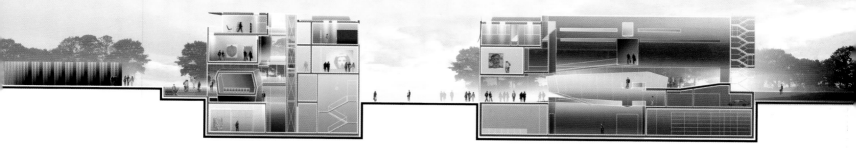

Color suffuses the buildings, giving them a brightness and vibrancy that would surely be lacking had everything been gray. Each space is used, with very little "lost" to architectural grandiloquence.

Farbe spielt bei dem Entwurf eine große Rolle und gibt den Räumen eine Helligkeit und Lebendigkeit, die bei reinen Grautönen sicherlich fehlen würden. Die Flächen werden gut genutzt, nur wenig Raum geht an architektonische Spielereien verloren.

La couleur qui baigne le bâtiment lui confère un éclat et une vibration dont il aurait sans doute manqué s'il était resté gris. Le moindre espace est utilisé et le tribut à la grandiloquence architecturale est minime.

3

JEAN-MARIE DUTHILLEUL

AREP
163 bis, avenue de Clichy
Impasse Chalabre
75847 Paris Cedex 17

Tel: +33 1 56 33 05 08
Fax: +33 1 56 33 04 16
e-mail: jean-marie.duthilleul@arep.fr
Web: www.arep.fr

Born in 1952, **JEAN-MARIE DUTHILLEUL** graduated from the prestigious École Polytechnique in Paris in 1975 and registered as an architect in 1979. He has been the co-head architect of the French National Railroads (SNCF) since 1986. His firms, the Agence des Gares, created in 1988, and AREP, created in 1997, are subsidiaries of the SNCF but have branched out well beyond the construction and renovation of French railway stations to build in several other countries. He has been instrumental in redefining the appearance of French railway stations and has had a broad influence in returning them to some degree of civility and brightness. He has renovated facilities, such as the Gare du Nord in Paris (1998–2002), and built numerous new stations, such as the Lille-Europe TGV Station, Lille (1988–94) or the Roissy TGV Station (1991–94, with Paul Andreu). More recently, Duthilleul designed the new TGV stations in Aix-en-Provence, Avignon and Valence (1998–2001). The Agence des Gares and AREP respectively employ 60 and 240 people. Since 2000, Jean-Marie Duthilleul has worked extensively in China on the Xizhimen Station, Beijing (2000–05); the Beijing Capital Museum (2001–05); and the Shanghai South Station (2001–06). Other projects include the Saint-François de Molitor Church, Paris (2004) and the TGV station in Torino, Italy (planned for 2009).

AVIGNON TGV STATION

AVIGNON
1998 - 2001

FLOOR AREA: 6641 m²
CLIENT: Direction des Gares SNCF
COST: €24.5 million

Located two kilometers from the historic Papal Palace of Avignon, the station is nonetheless set clearly outside the city's walled perimeter. Because of the topography of the site, the tracks arrive some seven meters above ground level. A long glass screen shelters passengers from the frequent Mistral winds on the northern platform. A form described by the architects as "an upturned stone hull" pierced with tall openings provides shelter from the sun opposite the Durance River, giving the 360-meter-long station a slightly introverted aspect. The long, covered southern platform provides a spectacular brightly lit interior space, and emphasizes the architects' desire to render any stay in the station a pleasant one. A long, generously planted avenue links the station to the city itself, setting the tone for future urban development. Although greenery and pleasant views are amply provided for, the station does seem to be rather more distant from the town than might have been hoped.

Der Bahnhof liegt nur 2 km vom Papstpalast in Avignon entfernt, aber dennoch deutlich außerhalb der Stadtmauern. Aufgrund der Topografie verlaufen die Gleise circa 7 m über dem normalen Geländeniveau. Auf dem nördlichen Bahnsteig schützt eine lange Glaswand die Fahrgäste vor dem häufig wehenden Mistral. Die Form des Bahnhofs wird von den Architekten als »umgedrehter steinerner Schiffsrumpf« beschrieben. Die Außenhülle ist von hohen Öffnungen durchbrochen, sie fungiert als Sonnenschutz und verleiht dem 360 m langen Bahnhof am Ufer der Durance einen leicht introvertierten Charakter. Die Überbauung des südlichen Bahnsteigs bietet einen spektakulären, sehr hellen Innenraum und entspricht dem Anliegen der Architekten, für einen angenehmen Aufenthalt in diesem Bahnhof zu sorgen. Eine lange, großzügig bepflanzte Allee verbindet den Bahnhof mit der Innenstadt und gibt den Ton für die zukünftige städtebauliche Entwicklung an. Obwohl für reichlich Begrünung und angenehme Ausblicke gesorgt wurde, scheint der Bahnhof weiter entfernt von der Stadt zu sein, als man es sich erhofft hatte.

Située à deux kilomètres du palais des Papes en Avignon, la gare est implantée hors des remparts de la cité. Du fait de la topographie, les voies se trouvent à quelque sept mètres au-dessus du sol. Sur le quai nord, un long écran de verre abrite les voyageurs du mistral, fréquent. Une forme présentée par les architectes comme « une coque de pierre renversée », ponctuée de hautes trouées verticales, les protège du soleil face à la Durance et donne à cette gare de 360 m de long un aspect légèrement introverti. Le quai sud, couvert, bénéficie d'un spectaculaire volume intérieur généreusement éclairé qui témoigne du désir de l'agence de rendre plus agréable le temps passé en gare. Une longue avenue plantée, futur axe de développement urbain, relie la gare au centre ville. Si la verdure et les vues agréables sont très présentes, la gare semble cependant plus éloignée de la ville qu'on aurait pu l'espérer.

The intervention of Duthilleul and his colleagues includes not only the architecture of the station itself but also the immediate environment. Naturally, in the case of such a large project, the expertise of many, in particular those who are specialized in high-speed trains, is necessary.

Der Eingriff Duthilleuls und seiner Kollegen umfasst nicht nur den Bahnhof, sondern auch dessen direktes Umfeld. Wie immer bei Projekten dieser Größe werden die Fachkenntnisse vieler Experten – und in diesem Fall besonders die der Spezialisten für Hochgeschwindigkeitszüge – benötigt.

L'intervention de Duthilleul et de ses confrères comprenait à la fois l'architecture de la gare et son environnement immédiat. Pour un projet de cet ampleur, l'expertise de tous est nécessaire, en particulier celle des spécialistes des trains à grande vitesse.

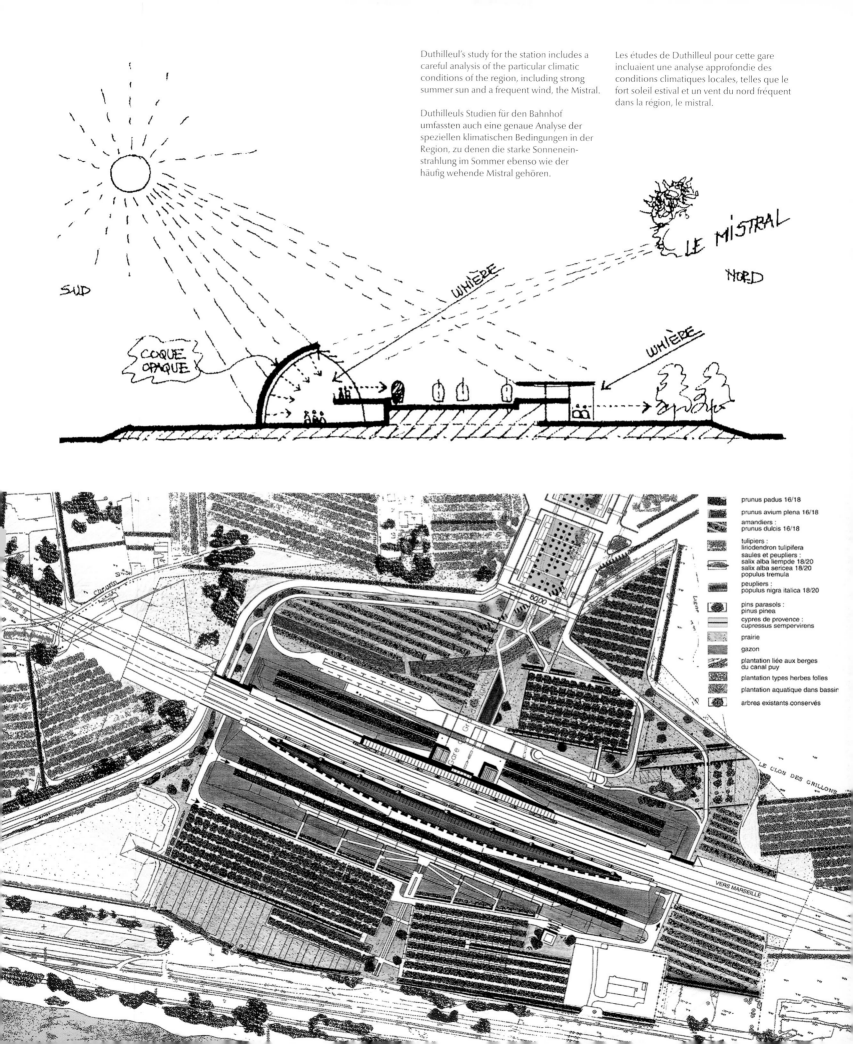

Duthilleul's study for the station includes a careful analysis of the particular climatic conditions of the region, including strong summer sun and a frequent wind, the Mistral.

Duthilleuls Studien für den Bahnhof umfassten auch eine genaue Analyse der speziellen klimatischen Bedingungen in der Region, zu denen die starke Sonnenein-strahlung im Sommer ebenso wie der häufig wehende Mistral gehören.

Les études de Duthilleul pour cette gare incluaient une analyse approfondie des conditions climatiques locales, telles que le fort soleil estival et un vent du nord fréquent dans la région, le mistral.

SUD

LE MISTRAL

NORD

WHIÈRE

WHIÈRE

COQUE OPAQUE

prunus padus 16/18
prunus avium plena 16/18
amandiers :
prunus dulcis 16/18
tulipiers :
liriodendron tulipifera
saules et peupliers :
salix alba liempde 18/20
salix alba sericea 18/20
populus tremula
peupliers :
populus nigra italica 18/20
pins parasols :
pinus pinea
cypres de provence :
cupressus sempervirens
prairie
gazon
plantation liée aux berges
du canal puy
plantation types herbes folles
plantation aquatique dans bassin
arbres existants conservés

VERS MARSEILLE

LE CLOS DES GRILLONS

ST FRANÇOIS DE MOLITOR CHURCH

PARIS 2001 · 05

FLOOR AREA: 1392 m² – Church 400 m²
CLIENT: Association Diocésaine de Paris
COST: €3 million

A catholic chapel that was built in 1941 in the 16th arrondissement of Paris on the rue Molitor was judged too small and structurally unsound in 1985. Having been until 1996 part of the parish of Notre Dame d'Auteuil, Saint-François de Molitor became a parish in its own right with 1500 members at that date. This project, the result of a 1991 competition, involved the construction of a church and a parish hall. The nave of the church is conceived like a hollowed-out space or the hull of a ship and its oval walls are likened by the architects to two hands cupped to receive water. The centrally placed altar is somewhat unusual in terms of liturgical traditions, but it works well with the curved forms of the nave. A garden, representing the Garden of Eden, is visible from within the church. Three large wooden doors and a bell tower give more traditional signs of the presence of a church from the street.

1985 wurden an der 1941 in der Rue Molitor im 16. Arrondissement von Paris gebauten katholischen Kapelle statische Mängel festgestellt; außerdem befand man sie für zu klein. Bis 1996 gehörte sie zum Pfarrbezirk Notre Dame d'Auteuil, danach wurde sie unter dem Namen Saint-François de Molitor selbstständiger Pfarrbezirk mit zu dem Zeitpunkt 1500 Mitgliedern. Das Projekt, Ergebnis eines Wettbewerbs aus dem Jahr 1991, umfasst das Kirchengebäude sowie einen Saal für die Gemeindemitglieder. Der Kirchenraum ähnelt einem ausgehöhlten Schiffsrumpf; die auf einem ovalen Grundriss errichteten, gebogenen Wände wurden von den Architekten mit zwei hohlen Händen verglichen, in die Wasser gegossen wird. Der zentral angeordnete Altar entspricht nicht unbedingt der liturgischen Tradition, scheint aber innerhalb der gebogenen Wände gut zu funktionieren. Vom Kirchenraum blickt man in einen Garten, der den Garten Eden symbolisiert. Zur Straße hin geben drei große Holztüren und ein Glockenturm eher traditionelle Hinweise auf das Vorhandensein einer Kirche.

Édifiée en 1941 dans le XVIᵉ arrondissement de Paris, rue Molitor, cette chapelle catholique était devenue trop petite et commençait à poser des problèmes de sécurité. Rattachée à la paroisse de Notre-Dame d'Auteuil jusqu'en 1996, Saint-François-de-Molitor est ensuite devenue une paroisse autonome de mille cinq cents fidèles. Le concours organisé en 1991 portait sur la construction d'une église et d'une salle paroissiale. La nef est un espace creusé, une « nef de bateau » dont les murs ovales sont comparés par les architectes à deux mains réunies en coupe pour recevoir de l'eau. Le positionnement central de l'autel est assez rare dans la liturgie catholique mais semble bien s'accorder à la forme ovale de la nef. Le jardin, symbole du Jardin d'Eden, est visible depuis l'intérieur de l'église. Côté rue, trois grandes portes en bois et un clocher constituent des signaux plus traditionnels de la présence d'une église.

The relatively austere church exterior gives way to a warmer interior, where the arrangement of the pews evokes the image of cupped hands. A sketch shows the north-south axial alignment of the church, which is located between the garden and the city.

Das eher strenge Äußere der Kirche kontrastiert mit dem warmen Innenraum, in dem die Anordnung der Kirchenbänke das Bild hohler Hände evoziert. Eine Skizze verdeutlicht die präzise axiale Anordnung der Kirche zwischen Garten und Stadt sowie die Ausrichtung in Nord-Süd-Richtung.

L'extérieur de l'église relativement austère laisse place à l'intérieur à un volume plus chaleureux : le thème des mains jointes en position d'offrande y est ainsi évoqué dans la disposition des bancs. Le croquis montre l'alignement axial précis de l'église entre le jardin et la ville, et surtout entre le nord et le sud.

The interior space of the church is at once warm and carefully worked out in terms of its liturgical requirements, even if Duthilleul's plan is not a conventional cruciform design.

Das Innere der Kirche wirkt warm und ist mit Rücksicht auf die liturgischen Erfordernisse sorgfältig ausgearbeitet, auch wenn der Entwurf von Duthilleul keinen konventionellen kreuzförmigen Grundriss aufweist.

L'église est à la fois accueillante et soigneusement pensée en fonction de la liturgie. Néanmoins, elle ne relève pas de la tradition des plans cruciformes.

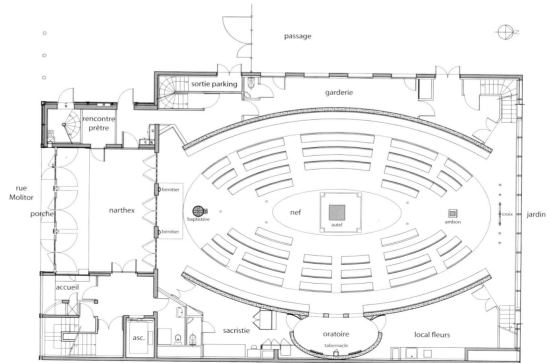

4

EDOUARD FRANÇOIS

EDOUARD FRANÇOIS
136, rue Falguière
75015 Paris

Tel: +33 1 45 67 88 87
Fax: +33 1 45 67 51 45
e-mail: agence@edouardfrancois.com
Web: www.edouardfrancois.com

EDOUARD FRANÇOIS was born in Paris in 1957 and educated as an architect and urban designer. He attended the Beaux-Arts in Paris and the École National des Ponts et Chaussées, becoming an architect in 1983. He has taught at the École National Supérieure du Paysage in Versailles (1998–99); the Architectural Association (AA) in London (1997–98) and the École Spéciale d'Architecture in Paris the same year. The work of Edouard François emphasizes sustainable design and direct relations with nature. He completed the extension and renovation of the Buffon Primary School in Thiais, France (1996); an apartment building called « L'Immeuble qui Pousse » (the Building that Grows—a structure covered in a mesh of steel cages containing loosely compacted stones in which plants can grow) in Montpellier (2000); the covering for a ventilation tower in La Défense, Paris (2004); and the Palace Fouquet's Barrière hotel in Paris (2006). Current work includes the renovation and extension of the Ternes Parking facility in Paris (2007).

TOWER FLOWER
PARIS
2001·03

FLOOR AREA: 2600 m²
CLIENT: OPAC, Paris
COST: €4 million

Located in the ZAC or development area of the Porte d'Asnières in Paris, which was laid out by Christian de Portzamparc, this unusual building features more than 380 large suspended planters, all of which are automatically watered. Two bamboos are planted in each pot, though every apartment is allotted one unplanted pot for use at the tenant's discretion. There are 30 apartments on nine levels plus three levels of underground parking. "A long time ago," says the architect, "I made a proposal to a Paris promoter. I told him I thought that gardens and buildings should be conceived as one. I imagined buildings that would be a pendant to parks planted with the same flowers and trees—a park that would look up to 'forested' façades. Inside each residence, the plants filter the city to escape it, to establish a distance with it and to minimize its density, giving one the impression of living in a natural setting." Although some may find the idea of suspending planters from an otherwise quite normal building extravagant or humorous, Edouard François's commitment to sustainable design and environmentally conscious structures makes his Tower Flower an interesting contribution to the city of Paris where, as he points out, balcony gardens of various types are everywhere in evidence.

Das ungewöhnliche Gebäude liegt in dem von Christian de Portzamparc konzipierten Entwicklungsgebiet Porte d'Asnières (ZAC) in Paris. Besonderes Kennzeichen dieses Wohnhauses sind die über 380 großen Blumentöpfe, die automatisch bewässert werden. Die Töpfe sind mit jeweils zwei Bambussträuchern bepflanzt; zu jedem Appartement gehört aber auch noch ein Topf, der von den Bewohnern selbst individuell bepflanzt werden kann. In dem neungeschossigen Hochhaus gibt es 30 Appartements, hinzu kommen drei Tiefgaragengeschosse. »Es ist schon lange her«, so der Architekt, »dass ich einem Pariser Immobilienpromotor einen Vorschlag machte. Ich sagte ihm, Gärten und Gebäude sollten als Einheit entworfen sein. Ich stellte mir Gebäude als Pendants zu Parks vor, mit den gleichen Blumen und Bäumen bepflanzt, oder anders gesagt, einen Park, der zu

›bewaldeten‹ Fassaden gewissermaßen hinaufblicken würde. In den Wohnungen sollten die Pflanzen die Stadt filtern und das Gefühl vermitteln, in einer natürlichen Umgebung zu leben.« Manche werden die Idee, Blumentöpfe an einem ansonsten eher alltäglichen Gebäude anzubringen für extravagant oder humorig halten, aber Edouard François' Engagement für nachhaltige Architektur und umweltbewusste Konstruktionen machen seinen Flower Tower zu einem interessanten Beitrag in Paris, einer Stadt, in der (darauf verweist der Architekt) Balkongärten unterschiedlicher Art überall zu finden sind.

Situé dans la ZAC de la Porte d'Asnières à Paris aménagée selon un plan d'urbanisme de Christian de Portzamparc, cet immeuble étonnant exhibe trois cent quatre-vingts grands pots de fleurs arrosés automatiquement. La plupart sont garnis de deux bambous, mais chaque appartement dispose d'un pot vide à planter à sa convenance. L'immeuble compte trente appartements sur neuf étages et trois niveaux de parkings souterrains. « Il y a longtemps », explique l'architecte, « j'ai fais une proposition, à un aménageur Parisien, de jardins et d'immeubles, qui devaient être conçus à l'unisson. J'avais imaginé les immeubles comme des pendants du parc, plantés des mêmes essences. Un parc sans vis-à-vis donnant sur des façades ›forêts‹. Côté intérieur, côté logement, cela donnait au premier plan des filtres de nature qui de proche en proche s'épaississaient pour vous donner l'impression d'habiter en pleine nature. » Bien que certains puissent trouver extravagante ou humoristique cette idée de garnir de pots de fleurs la façade par ailleurs assez classique d'un immeuble, l'engagement d'Edouard François en faveur du développement durable et de l'architecture environnementale font de cette « Tour aux fleurs » une intéressante contribution à la ville de Paris où, comme il le fait remarquer, l'on peut voir des balcons-jardins de types variés un peu partout.

The aligned planters of the tower correspond to the frequently avowed love affair of Parisians with terrace plants but, in this instance, also echo the neighboring park. By lining up identical pots, the architect has created a strong urban presence, where the idea might have easily gone wrong.

Die in Reihen angeordneten Blumentöpfe stehen im Einklang mit der allseits bekannten Liebe der Pariser zu Balkonpflanzen, beziehen sich in diesem Fall aber auch auf den benachbarten Park. Durch die Anordnung gleicher Töpfe schafft der Architekt eine starke urbane Präsenz; die Idee hätte auch leicht schief gehen können

Les rangées de pots de fleurs répondent au goût des Parisiens pour les terrasses plantées, mais ici, elles font également référence au parc voisin. Avec ces alignements de pots identiques, l'architecte a créé un objet urbain à la forte présence, idée qui aurait pu facilement manquer son but si elle avait été mal maîtrisée.

5

MANUELLE GAUTRAND

**MANUELLE GAUTRAND
ARCHITECTE**
36, boulevard de la Bastille
75012 Paris

Tel: +33 1 56 95 06 46
Fax: +33 1 56 95 06 47
e-mail: contact@manuelle-gautrand.com
Web: www.manuelle-gautrand.com

Born in 1961, **MANUELLE GAUTRAND** received her architecture degree in 1985. She founded her own office in 1991. She has been a teacher at the École Spéciale d'Architecture in Paris (1999–2000), at the Paris-Val-de-Seine University (2000–03), and participates in numerous student workshops outside of France. In 2001, she was selected to participate in the limited competition for the François Pinault Contemporary Art Museum that was to be located on the Île Seguin near Paris. Her built work includes a 72-meter-long pedestrian bridge, Lyon (1993); five highway toll booths (in the Somme region on the A16 freeway, 1998); the Theater of the National Center for Dramatic Arts, Béthune (1998); an Airport Catering Center, Nantes (1999); and an Institute of Technology at Meulun-Sénart University (1999). Aside from the Espace Citroën, Paris (2003–06), her current work includes the Administrative Center, Saint-Étienne (2005–07); "Solaris," a 100-unit sustainable apartment building, Rennes (2006); the extension and restructuring of the Lille Museum of Contemporary Art (2007); a cultural complex, Rambouillet (2007); the "Gaîté Lyrique" Digital Arts and Music Center, Paris (2008); the refurbishment of the "Paris Department Store," Budapest (2008); an office building, Amsterdam (2008); and, in association with Kieler Architect, a mixed housing-office and retail program in Copenhagen, Denmark (2008). She works with her partner, Marc Blaising, and a permanent staff of 15 architects.

ADMINISTRATIVE CENTER SAINT-ÉTIENNE 2005 - 07

FLOOR AREA: 27 000 m²
CLIENT: Cogedim-Ric / JFP Participations
COST: €35 million

This site is considered an entry point to the new area of Chateaucreux in Saint-Étienne and is intended for a variety of government services. A restaurant, café and tourist office are included in the complex. The architecture is conceived as a long "continuum," from one adjacent street to the other. The generous main entrance on the avenue Grüner side with its cantilevered volume guides visitors into the building. Two other large openings allow pedestrians to circulate through and around the large building. The "continuum" concept gives an architectural unity to the Center but also permits the administrations that occupy it to expand or contract as circumstances require. They do not occupy set parts of the building, but can take advantage of its flexibility. The building has three silvery glazed façades and one opaque bright yellow side. The yellow surfaces are meant to generate a warm glow. As the architects say, "The project is also about a meeting between gray and yellow, silver and gold."

Das Grundstück markiert einen der Zugänge zu Saint-Étiennes neuem Stadtteil Châteaucreux. Hier sollen eine Reihe staatlicher Einrichtungen und Dienste angesiedelt werden, außerdem ein Restaurant, ein Café und eine Touristeninformation. Das Gebäude ist als »Kontinuum« zwischen zwei Straßen gedacht. Der großzügige Haupteingang an der avenue Grüner mit seinem auskragenden Volumen leitet die Besucher in das Gebäude. Zwei weitere große Öffnungen erleichtern die Erschließung zu Fuß durch und um das Gebäude herum. Das Konzept des Kontinuums bedingt eine architektonische Einheit des Komplexes, gleichzeitig erlaubt es den verschiedenen Verwaltungsabteilungen, sich je nach Bedarf zu vergrößern oder zu verkleinern. Die Abteilungen sind nicht bestimmten Teilen des Gebäudes zugeordnet, sondern können seine Flexibilität nutzen. Die Hauptfassaden des Gebäudes bestehen aus silbrigem Glas, die Fassaden der Einschnitte haben eine opake, leuchtend gelbe Farbe. Die gelben Oberflächen sollen ein warmes Schimmern erzeugen. Dazu die Architekten: »Thema des Projekts ist auch das Zusammentreffen von Grau und Gelb, Silber und Gold.«

Ce site, qui doit accueillir divers services administratifs, est comme une porte d'entrée dans le nouveau quartier de Chateaucreux, à Saint-Étienne. L'ensemble doit comprendre également l'Office du tourisme, un restaurant et un café. L'architecture est conçue comme long « continuum » entre deux rues. L'importante entrée à volume en porte-à-faux sur l'avenue Grüner oriente les visiteurs vers le bâtiment et deux autres grandes ouvertures permettent aux piétons de circuler aisément autour du complexe. Le concept de continuum assure l'unité architecturale du Centre et fait que les administrations qui l'occuperont pourront s'agrandir ou se rétracter selon les circonstances. Elles n'occupent pas des parties définies de l'immeuble, mais bénéficient de sa souplesse d'aménagement. L'immeuble présente trois façades vitrées réfléchissantes et une opaque, jaune vif, sur le côté, qui devrait réverbérer une lumière chaleureuse. Pour les architectes, « le projet est aussi une rencontre entre des couleurs, le gris et le jaune, l'or et l'argent ».

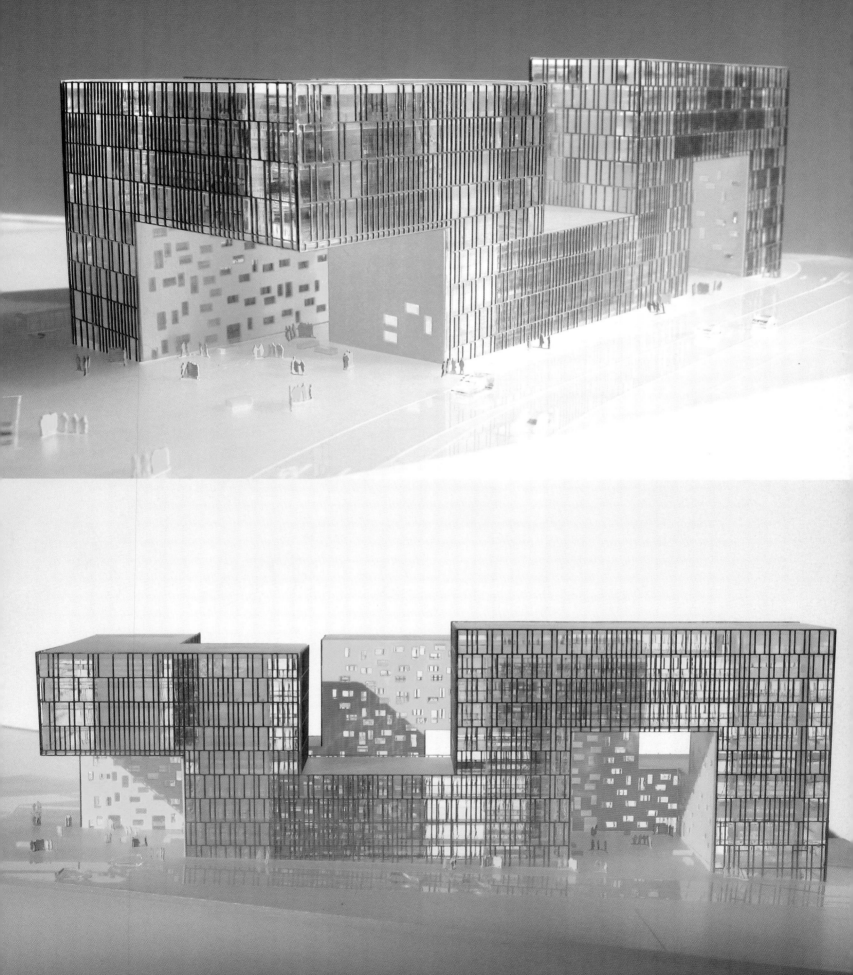

A meandering pattern of cutouts and openings assures that the large structure retains a high degree of potential exposure to the exterior and ample natural light where required. The floor plans below reveal the regularity of the design.

Einschnitte und Öffnungen bilden ein mäanderähnliches Muster. Das große Gebäude erhält auf diese Weise einen vielfältigen Bezug zum Außenraum und wird, wo nötig, sehr gut natürlich belichtet. Der Grundriss unten zeigt die Regelmäßigkeit des Entwurfs.

Les lignes sinueuses des découpes et des ouvertures permettent à cette vaste construction de bénéficier d'un généreux éclairage naturel là où cela est nécessaire. Les plans des étages, ci-dessous, révèlent la composition régulière qui sous-tend le projet.

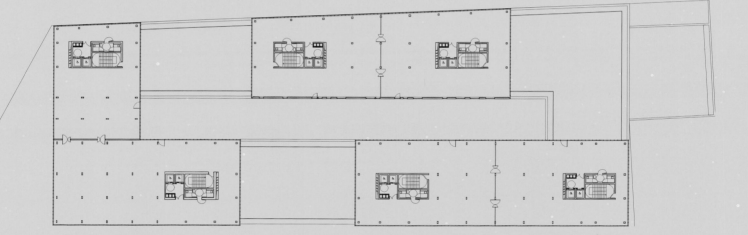

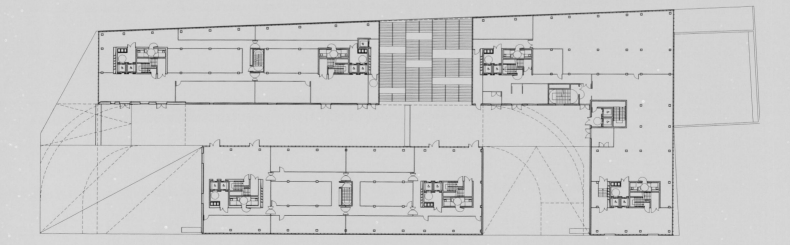

The zigzag pattern imposed by the architect is seen both in plan and in section in these images. The use of a bright yellow heightens the visibility of the cutouts. Modernist rectilinearity is undermined and yet remains in the disposition of usable spaces.

Sowohl im Grundriss als auch im Schnitt tritt das übergeordnete Zickzackmuster hervor. Das kräftige Gelb erhöht die Sichtbarkeit der Einschnitte. Die Rechtwinkligkeit der Moderne wird unterlaufen, bleibt aber in der Anordnung der Nutzflächen erhalten.

Le motif en zigzag imposé par l'architecte apparaît ici aussi bien sur le plan qu'en coupe. L'utilisation du jaune vif souligne les découpes. La composition rectiligne d'esprit moderniste, sous-jacente, est décelable dans la répartition des espaces.

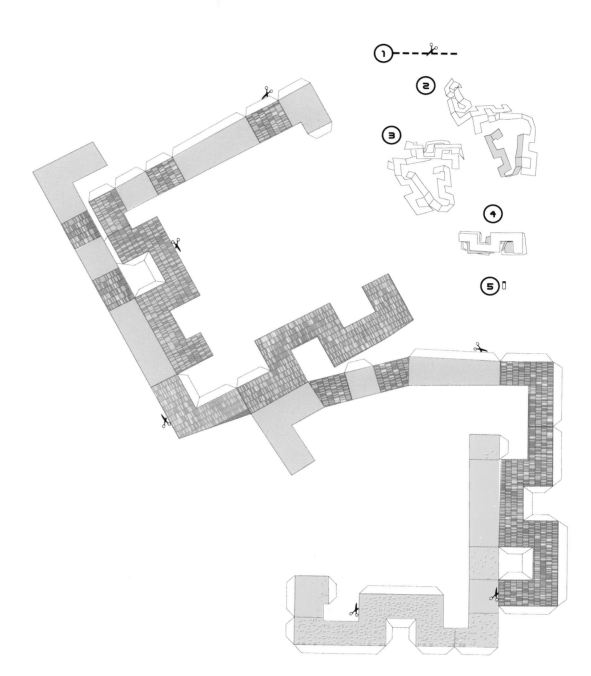

ESPACE CITROËN
PARIS
2003-06

FLOOR AREA: 1200 m²
CLIENT: Citroën, PSA Group
COST: €11 million

The car manufacturer Citroën installed a showroom at number 42, Champs-Élysées, in 1927. Four years later, the firm called on its factory designer Ravazé and its own art director Pierre Louys to redo the building in a style judged befitting of the brand until 1984. Home to a restaurant for the next years, the Citroën showroom had become outdated and the company decided in 2002 to organize an international design competition with such participants as Zaha Hadid, Daniel Libeskind and Christian de Portzamparc. The winner was the young French architect Manuelle Gautrand, who was to rebuild the 1200 m² structure. Using the inverted double-V symbol of the firm, Gautrand designed a complex glass façade that reveals successive platforms where Citroën vehicles are to be exhibited. She makes subtle reference to the previous Art-Deco façade of the showroom that was so long admired. Her intention is that the interior platforms should not only be moveable but also actually turn slowly. The platform system permits a full use of the considerable interior height while not actually breaking up the space. The architect took as her cue words of the car designer Pininfarina, who stated that "Citroën means non-aggressive performance..." But performance nonetheless.

Im Jahr 1927 bezog der Autohersteller Citroën einen Showroom auf den Champs-Élysées 42. Vier Jahre später beauftragte das Unternehmen seinen Industriedesigner Ravazé und seinen Artdirector Pierre Louys, das Gebäude in einem Stil umzugestalten, der bis ins Jahr 1984 als zu der Automarke passend galt. Nachdem der ehemalige Citroën-Showroom, der dann ein Restaurant beherbergte, unmodern geworden war, beschloss die Firmenleitung 2002, einen internationalen Wettbewerb zu organisieren, an dem unter anderem Zaha Hadid, Daniel Libeskind und Christian de Portzamparc teilnahmen. Siegerin wurde jedoch die junge französische Architektin Manuelle Gautrand, die das gesamte, 1200 m² umfassende Gebäude umbauen sollte. Unter Verwendung des Firmensignets – das umgekehrte Doppel-V – entwarf Gautrand eine komplex strukturierte Glasfassade, durch die

man die übereinander angeordneten Plattformen, auf denen die Citroën-Modelle präsentiert werden, erkennen kann. Dabei stellt sie einen raffinierten Bezug zu der einst so bewunderten Art déco Fassade des Autogeschäfts her. Ihre Absicht ist außerdem, dass die Plattformen im Innenraum nicht nur beweglich sind, sondern sich auch noch langsam um die eigene Achse drehen. Dieses Bühnensystem erlaubt die volle Nutzung der beträchtlichen Höhe des Gebäudes, ohne den Raum selbst zu zerteilen. Die Architektin richtete sich bei ihrer Gestaltung nach den Worten des Autodesigners Pininfarina, der einmal sagte: »Citroën bedeutet unaggressive Leistung.« Nichtsdestoweniger eine Leistung.

Le constructeur automobile Citroën a installé son premier magasin au 42, avenue des Champs-Élysées en 1927. En 1931, il fit appel à son designer Ravazé et à son directeur artistique Pierre Louys pour reconstruire l'immeuble dans un style qui exprima la marque avec pertinence jusqu'en 1984. Un nouveau showroom Citroën accouplé à un restaurant est alors réaménagé, mais se démode assez vite. En 2002, le constructeur a lancé un concours international qui réunit des participants comme Zaha Hadid, Daniel Libeskind et Christian de Portzamparc. Il fut remporté par la jeune architecte française Manuelle Gautrand, chargée de reconstruire entièrement cette structure de 1200 m². Utilisant le double chevron symbole de la firme, elle a conçu une façade complexe en verre qui mettra en valeur diverses plates-formes sur lesquelles seront exposés des véhicules, dans une référence subtile à l'ancienne façade Art Déco longtemps admirée. Les plates-formes intérieures devraient être à la fois mobiles et tourner lentement sur elles-mêmes. Ce système permettra d'utiliser pleinement la considérable hauteur du volume intérieur sans le rompre pour autant. Gautrand a pris au mot ce commentaire du designer automobile Pininfarina disant que « Citroën signifie performance non agressive... ».

The picture of the façade on the Champs-Élysées on the left-hand page was taken in the course of construction in the spring of 2006. A section and perspectives show how the cars will be displayed on turning platforms suspended in the large open interior space.

Das Foto der Fassade an den Champs-Élysées wurde während der Bauzeit im Frühjahr 2006 aufgenommen. Schnitt und Perspektiven zeigen, wie die Automobile auf den sich drehenden, im großen Innenraum abgehängten Plattformen präsentiert werden sollen.

La photographie de la façade sur les Champs-Élysées a été prise pendant le chantier, au printemps 2006. Une coupe et des perspectives montrent la future présentation des voitures sur des plates-formes pivotantes suspendues dans le vaste volume intérieur.

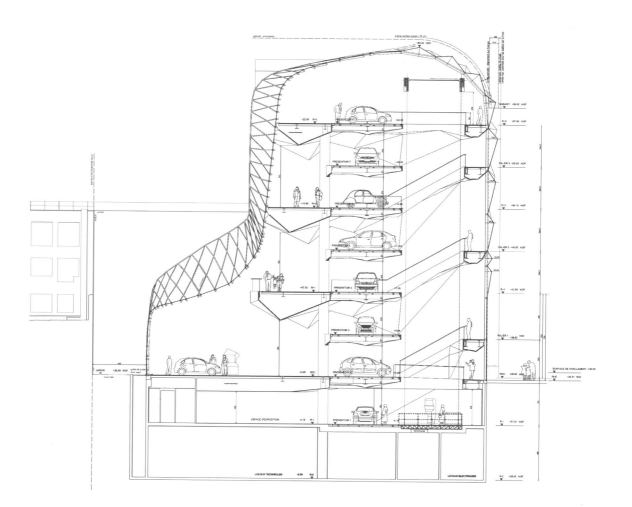

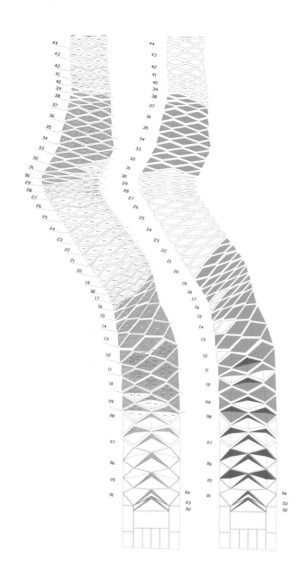

The architect has used a highly stylized version of the car manufacturer's double chevron symbol to animate her design, from the façade to the interior.

Um ihren Entwurf zu beleben, verwendete die Architektin sowohl bei der Fassade als auch im Innenraum eine stark stilisierte Version des doppelten Winkelsymbols des Autoherstellers.

L'architecte s'est servi d'une version très stylisée du double-chevron, symbole du constructeur, pour animer le projet, de la façade vers l'intérieur.

LILLE MUSEUM OF MODERN ART EXTENSION
VILLENEUVE D'ASCQ
2004 - 08

FLOOR AREA: 9000 m^2
CLIENT: Lille Metropole Communauté Urbaine
COST: €11 million

Designed by the architect Roland Simounet (1927–96), the Lille Museum of Modern Art (1978–83) is presently being expanded by Manuelle Gautrand. Her extension, inscribed "in the space available between the existing building and the limits of the property [is] a long, complex volume that freely develops its extremities to respond to very different needs: services near the technical premises to the west, and exhibition rooms toward the Parc des Sculptures. Like an (organic) ramification, in a single movement the most diverse components—even the basement-level reserves—merge into an arrangement that is shaped primarily by internal events." Gautrand has been careful not to conflict with Simounet's well regarded design while solving a number of its functional problems. She describes her building as being an "outgrowth, in the form of a hand or a root... an emanation of the topography, as much as a free development that is topological in essence." She has adapted her work to the circumstances, making a limited extension of Simounet's grid for the contemporary art rooms, creating space for Art Brut that is "close to the soil and plant life" as well as meeting the low natural light requirements imposed in this area by the curators.

Das Musée d'Art Moderne (1978–83), entworfen von Roland Simounet (1927–96), wird nach Plänen von Manuelle Gautrand vergrößert. Die Erweiterung, eingeschrieben »in den zur Verfügung stehenden Raum zwischen dem bestehenden Gebäude und den Grundstücksgrenzen, [ist] ein langer, komplexer Baukörper, dessen ›Extremitäten‹ sich frei entwickeln, um auf die sehr unterschiedlichen Anforderungen zu reagieren: Die Serviceeinrichtungen liegen in der Nähe der technischen Bereiche im Westen, die Ausstellungsräume zum Parc des Sculptures. Wie bei einer [organischen] Verzweigung fließen in einer Bewegung die unterschiedlichsten Komponenten - sogar die Raumreserven im Untergeschoss - in einer Anordnung zusammen, die in erster Linie durch Ereignisse im Inneren bestimmt wird.« Gautrand hat sorgfältig vermieden, einen Gegensatz zu Simounets

allgemein geschätztem Gebäude zu schaffen und gleichzeitig eine Reihe seiner funktionalen Probleme gelöst. Sie beschreibt ihr Gebäude als »Auswuchs, in Form einer Hand oder einer Wurzel ... etwas, das die Topografie ›ausströmte‹, ebenso wie etwas frei Entwickeltes, das im Grundsatz topologisch ist«. Der Entwurf ist den Umständen angepasst: Simounets Raster wurde für die Räume für zeitgenössische Kunst begrenzt erweitert, Raum für die Art Brut, der »dicht am Erdreich und am Pflanzenleben ist,« geschaffen, und auch den Anforderungen der Kuratoren nach niedriger Beleuchtungsintensität in diesem Bereich entsprochen.

Conçu par l'architecte Roland Simounet (1927–96), le musée d'Art moderne de Lille, à Villeneuve-d'Ascq (1978–83), est en cours d'extension. Le projet de Manuelle Gautrand, inscrit « dans l'espace disponible entre les bâtiments existants et les limites du terrain, [est] un volume allongé complexe qui se développe librement à ses extrémités pour répondre à différents besoins : services et installations techniques à l'ouest, salles d'exposition vers le parc des Sculptures. Comme une ramification naturelle, les composants les plus variés (y compris les réserves en sous-sol) fusionnent en un seul mouvement dans une disposition qui est essentiellement la résultante de ce qui se passe à l'intérieur. » M. Gautrand a pris soin de ne pas entrer en conflit avec les bâtiments de Simounet dont la qualité est appréciée, tout en s'efforçant de résoudre les quelques problèmes fonctionnels qu'ils posaient. L'architecte décrit son projet comme « une excroissance, en forme de main ou de racine... une émanation de la topographie autant qu'un développement libre, topologique par essence ». Elle a adapté son travail au contexte en créant, pour l'art contemporain, une petite extension de la trame des salles d'exposition prévue par Simounet, ainsi qu'un espace pour l'art brut, « proche du sol et de la vie végétale », qui respecte les normes d'éclairage réduit imposées par les conservateurs pour ce type de département.

Drawings and a model show how Gautrand has brought a freer form to the existing, complex accumulation of boxes that forms the museum. Despite the apparently unusual form of her extension, a site plan shows that she is sensitive to the existing urban pattern.

Zeichnungen und das Modell zeigen die freiere Form, um die Gautrand die bestehende, komplexe Anordnung von »Kisten«, die das Museum bilden, erweitert hat. Der Lageplan veranschaulicht die sensible Eingliederung in die bestehende städtebauliche Ordnung.

Dessins et maquette montrent comment Manuelle Gautrand a donné une forme plus libre à l'accumulation complexe de boîtes qui constitue le musée. Un plan du site prouve que cette extension est parfaitement adaptée au tissu urbain.

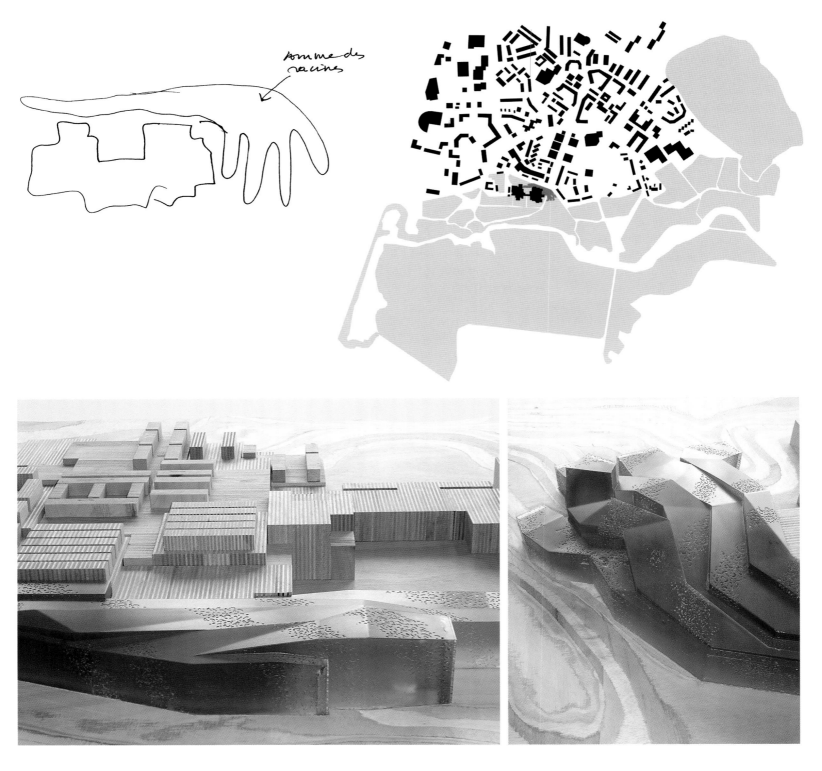

The blue volumes seen in the model and the drawings add a dynamic sensuality to shapes that otherwise might appear to be industrial in their accumulation and regularity. It might not be "sexist" to say that Manuelle Gautrand has brought a touch of femininity to the extension she designed.

Die im Modell und in den Zeichnungen dargestellten blauen Volumen ergänzen die ansonsten aufgrund ihrer Zahl und Regelmäßigkeit industriell erscheinenden Formen um eine dynamische und sinnliche Komponente. Es ist wohl nicht sexistisch zu sagen, dass Manuelle Gautrands Erweiterungsbau dadurch eine leicht feminine Note bekommt.

Les volumes bleus de la maquette et les dessins confèrent une sensualité dynamique à des formes qui, sans cela, auraient pu paraître « industrielles » dans leur accumulation et leur régularité. On pourrait dire, sans être taxé de sexisme, que Manuelle Gautrand a apporté une touche de féminité à cette extension.

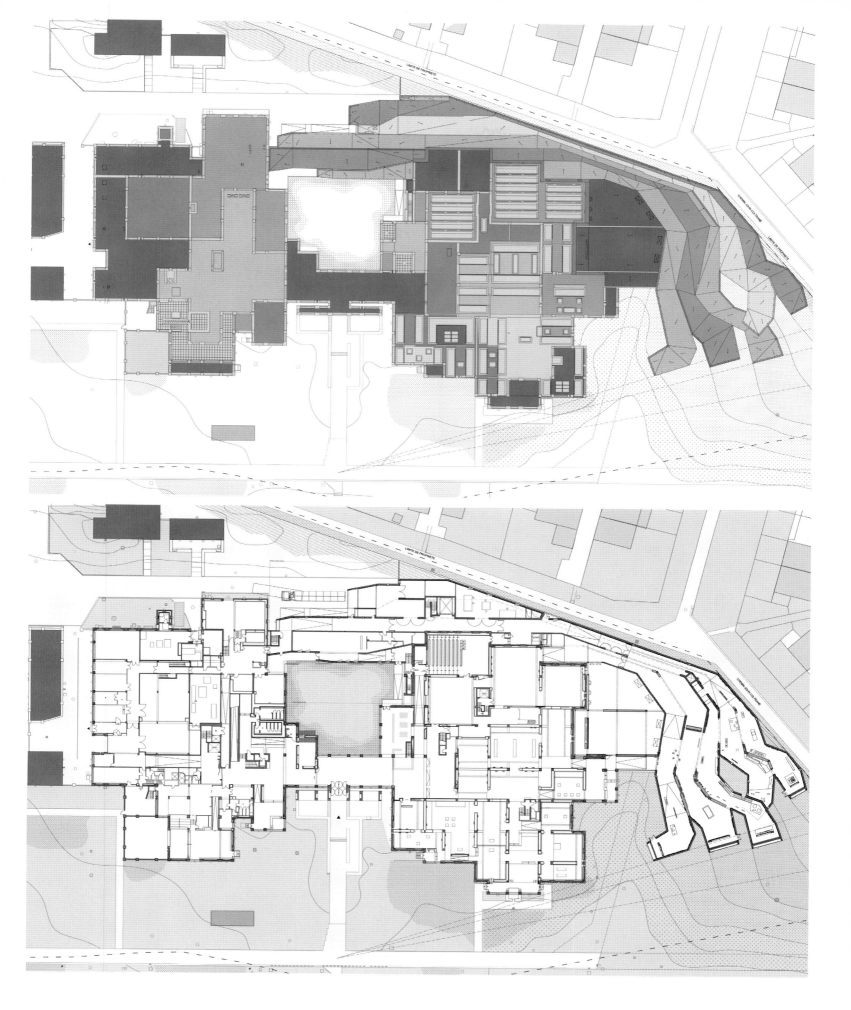

71

6

JAKOB + MACFARLANE

JAKOB + MACFARLANE
SARL D'ARCHITECTURE
13, rue des Petites Écuries
75010 Paris

Tel: +33 1 44 79 05 72
Fax: +33 1 48 00 97 93
e-mail: info@jakobmacfarlane.com
Web: www.jakobmacfarlane.com

DOMINIQUE JAKOB was born in 1966 and holds a degree in art history from the Université de Paris I (1990) and a degree in architecture from the École d'Architecture Paris-Villemin (1991). She has taught at the École Spéciale d'Architecture (1998–99) and at the École d'Architecture Paris-Villemin (1994–2000). Born in New Zealand in 1961, **BRENDAN MACFARLANE** received his Bachelor of Architecture at SCI-Arc, Los Angeles (1984), and his Master of Architecture degree at the Harvard Graduate School of Design (1990). He has taught at the Paris La Villette architecture school (1995–96), at the Berlage Institute, Amsterdam (1996), at the Bartlett School of Architecture in London (1996–98) and at the École Spéciale d'Architecture in Paris (1998–99). From 1995 to 1997, MacFarlane was an architectural critic at the Architectural Association (AA) in London. Jakob and MacFarlane founded their own agency in 1992 in Paris. Their main projects include the T House, La-Garenne-Colombes, France (1994–98); the Georges Restaurant at Georges Pompidou Center, Paris (1999–2000); the restructuring of the Maxime Gorki Theater, Petit-Quevilly, France (1999–2000) and the Renault International Communication Center, Boulogne (2002–05). They are currently working on the Saint-Nazaire Theater, France; the Herold housing complex in Paris, and the transformation of Parisian docks into a city of fashion and design (2005–08).

RENAULT SQUARE COM

BOULOGNE-BILLANCOURT 2002-05

FLOOR AREA: 14 500 m²
CLIENT: Régie Renault
COST: €23 million

In the early 1980s, the French automobile company Renault asked the architect Claude Vasconi to design about 20 new buildings to replace aging factory facilities located on the Séguin Island in the Seine at the western extremity of Paris, and on the right bank of the river. As it happens, he built only one structure, called Métal 57. Never used as a factory, Métal 57 has been converted by Jakob + MacFarlane into a communications center for Renault. With ceiling heights ranging between six and twelve meters, Métal 57 posed a challenge to the architects, intent on keeping something of the original spirit of the 150 00 m² building while turning it into a viable facility. Meant to be a place to base Renault's public relations staff of 250–300 employees, and to present new cars to the press and leaders in the automobile industry, the company envisioned a venue where its marketing groups from around the world could come for meetings, entertainment, dining and events showcasing its cars. Three auditoriums seating 100, 300 and 500 persons respectively were added to one side of the shed-like structure. Completed in 2005 for €23 million, the conversion successfully creates open, airy spaces ideally suited to showing cars. The architects partially lined the vast exhibition area with large, seven-centimeter-thick structural honeycomb panels faced in resin-coated aluminum. With exposed steel frames backing "pleated" white walls, the architects created display backdrops against which they can hang automobiles like works of art. As MacFarlane points out, "the wall material, made for aeronautics industry fuselages, is interesting because of its flatness and lightness."

In den frühen 1980er Jahren beauftragte der französische Autohersteller Renault den Architekten Claude Vasconi mit dem Entwurf von etwa 20 neuen Gebäuden als Ersatz für die in die Jahre gekommenen Fabrikanlagen auf der Seine-Insel Île Séguin im äußersten Westen von Paris und auf dem rechten Seineufer. Tatsächlich wurde aber nur einer dieser Entwürfe realisiert, das so genannte Métal-57-Gebäude. Métal 57 wurde jedoch nie als Werk benutzt und von Jakob + MacFarlane in ein Kommunikationszentrum für Renault umgebaut. Mit Deckenhöhen zwischen 6 und 12 m stellte Métal 57 eine Herausforderung für die Architekten dar: Einerseits wollten sie etwas von der ursprünglichen Atmosphäre des 150 00 m² großen Gebäudes erhalten, es aber andererseits in ein gut nutzbares Kommunikationszentrum verwandeln. 250 bis 300 Mitarbeiter der PR-Abteilung sollen hier arbeiten; außerdem dient es dazu, der Presse und wichtigen Personen der Automobilindustrie die neusten Modelle zu präsentieren. Renault stellte sich einen Ort vor, an dem seine Marketingteams aus der ganzen Welt für Meetings, Unterhal-

tungsveranstaltungen, Diners und andere Events, bei denen Autos vorgestellt werden, zusammenkommen. Drei Auditorien mit 100, 300 und 500 Plätzen wurden an der einen Seite des hallenartigen Baukörpers angefügt. 2005 wurde das 23 Millionen Euro teure Gebäude fertig gestellt. Mit dem Umbau ist es gelungen, offene, großzügige Räume zu schaffen, die sich ideal für die Präsentation von Autos eignen. Die riesigen Ausstellungsräume wurden z. T. mit großen, 7 cm dicken Paneelen mit einem Wabenkern und einer Oberfläche aus kunstharzbeschichtetem Aluminium ausgekleidet. Die Architekten entwarfen sichtbare Stahlkonstruktionen, die »gefältete« weiße Wände halten; an diesen Wänden können Automobile wie Kunstwerke aufgehängt werden. MacFarlane dazu: »Das Interessante am Material der Wand, das eigentlich zur Herstellung von Flugzeugrümpfen verwendet wird, ist seine glatte Oberfläche und sein geringes Gewicht.«

Au début des années 1980, le constructeur automobile Renault avait demandé à l'architecte Claude Vasconi de concevoir une vingtaine de bâtiments pour remplacer ses usines vieillissantes de l'île Seguin et de la rive droite de la Seine à Boulogne-Billancourt. Finalement, il ne réalisa qu'un seul bâtiment, appelé 57 Métal. Jamais utilisé en tant qu'usine, le lieu a été converti par Jakob + MacFarlane en Centre de communication Renault. L'ensemble, doté de plafonds de six à douze mètres de haut, représentait un défi pour les architectes, qui voulaient conserver en partie l'esprit d'origine de cette construction de 150 00 m² tout en la transformant en un équipement efficace. Ce lieu était destiné à accueillir les 250 à 300 personnes du département des relations presse de la firme et à présenter les nouveaux modèles aux journalistes et aux décideurs du secteur automobile. Renault prévoyait aussi d'y recevoir ses équipes de marketing du monde entier, qui pourraient s'y réunir, y travailler, se restaurer et assister à des événements organisés autour des voitures. Trois auditoriums de 100, 300 et 500 places sont venus se greffer au flanc de l'ancien bâtiment-hangar. Achevée en 2005 pour un budget de 23 millions d'euros, cette conversion a réussi à créer des espaces aérés et ouverts, parfaitement adaptés à leur fonction. Les architectes ont en partie habillé la vaste surface d'exposition de panneaux structurels en nid d'abeille d'aluminium de 7 cm d'épaisseur doublés de résine en façade. À partir d'une ossature apparente en acier qui soutient des murs blanc «plissés», ils ont créé des cimaises sur lesquelles sont accrochées les voitures, comme des œuvres d'art. Comme MacFarlane le fait remarquer, «ce matériau mural, fabriqué pour les fuselages d'avion, est intéressant pour sa légèreté et sa minceur».

Converting a building designed as an automobile factory into a communications center is no small feat—the only factor really working in the architects' favor was that the original architecture was well-designed and spacious.

Eine frühere Automobilfabrik in ein Kommunikationszentrum zu verwandeln, ist keine leichte Aufgabe – der einzige Faktor, der den Architekten half, war die Qualität und Großzügigkeit der ursprünglichen Architektur.

Transformer en centre de communication un bâtiment conçu pour être une usine de montage d'automobiles n'est pas une mince affaire. Les seuls atouts dont disposaient les architectes étaient la qualité et les dimensions généreuses de la construction d'origine.

With a relatively limited budget as compared to the vast floor area of the former factory, Brendan MacFarlane and Dominique Jakob succeeded in giving a future to an otherwise unused building. By accepting the industrial vocabulary of the architecture, they managed to convert it without undue expense and effort.

Im Vergleich zur immensen Grundfläche der ehemaligen Fabrik war das Budget relativ begrenzt. Brendan MacFarlane und Dominique Jakob ist es trotzdem gelungen, dem zuvor leer stehenden Bau eine Zukunft zu geben. Indem sie das Vokabular der Industriearchitektur akzeptierten, konnten sie das vorhandene Gebäude ohne hohe Kosten und übermäßigen Aufwand umbauen.

Pour un budget relativement limité au regard des vastes surfaces de l'ancienne usine, Brendan MacFarlane et Dominique Jakob sont parvenus à redonner un avenir à ce bâtiment abandonné. En prenant en compte le vocabulaire industriel existant, ils ont réussi cette conversion sans dépenses excessives ni efforts superflus.

The spaces closer to the auditoriums on one side of the building are treated in a more "elegant" way, with wood paneling and the same angled surfaces that characterize the entire renovation.

Die Räume in der Nähe der Vortragssäle auf der einen Seite des Gebäudes sind eleganter gestaltet. Sie erhielten eine Holzvertäfelung und die gleichen winkligen Oberflächen, die den gesamten Umbau kennzeichnen.

Sur l'un des côtés du bâtiment, les espaces proches de l'auditorium sont traités d'une façon plus sophistiquée, avec leurs murs lambrissés de bois et les mêmes plans inclinés qui caractérisent ce nouveau centre.

DOCKS DE PARIS CITY OF FASHION AND DESIGN

PARIS 2005-08

FLOOR AREA: 20 000 m²
CLIENT: Société éditrice de l'ICADE
COST: not disclosed

Located on the quai d'Austerlitz in the 13th arrondissement of Paris, this project aims to transform a 1907 industrial warehouse-type building made of concrete into a state-of-the-art showplace of fashion and design. Using a new lightweight glass construction system called "plug-over," the architects intend to modernize the building with forms inspired by the Seine River and its walkways. A panoramic rooftop terrace and a purpose-designed exterior lighting system will ensure that the new facility attracts attention at night as well as during the day. This project is part of the willful development of the areas (Seine Rive Gauche) around the French National Library, designed some years ago by Dominique Perrault. After their very visible Georges Restaurant on top of the Pompidou Center, Dominique Jakob and Brendan MacFarlane promise to leave their mark on Paris in an even more surprising way.

Das 1907 errichtete Lagerhaus aus Beton am Quai d'Austerlitz im 13. Arrondissement von Paris soll in einen zukunftsweisenden Ort für die Präsentation von Mode und Design umgewandelt werden. Bei der Modernisierung des Gebäudes ließen sich die Architekten von der Seine und ihren Uferwegen zu Formen inspirieren, die sie mithilfe des neuen leichten Verglasungssystems »plug-over« umsetzen. Eine Dachterrasse mit Panoramablick und eine speziell entwickelte Außenbe-leuchtung sollen sicherstellen, dass der neue Komplex ebenso bei Tag wie auch bei Nacht Aufmerksamkeit erregt. Das Haus ist Teil der angestrebten Entwicklung des Stadtteils Seine Rive Gauche um die Bibliothèque Nationale de France von Dominique Perrault. Dominique Jakob und Brendan MacFarlane haben mit ihrem Restaurant »Georges« auf dem Centre Pompidou bereits ein auffälliges Zeichen gesetzt. Mit diesem Projekt werden sie noch überraschendere Spuren in Paris hinterlassen.

Implanté sur le quai d'Austerlitz à Paris dans le XIIIe arrondissement, ce projet porte sur la conversion en vitrine de la mode et du design d'entrepôts en béton armé datant de 1907. Grâce à un nouveau système de construction légère en verre appelé « plug-over », les architectes proposent de moderniser l'ensemble avec des formes inspirées par la Seine et ses quais. Une terrasse panoramique sur le toit et un système d'éclairage extérieur programmable attireront l'attention aussi bien le jour que la nuit. Ce projet fait partie de la rénovation de la zone Rive-Gauche autour de la Bibliothèque nationale conçue il y a quelques années par Dominique Perrault. Après leur très visible restaurant Georges au sommet du Centre Pompidou, Dominique Jakob et Brendan MacFarlane laisseront là une empreinte encore plus surprenante sur le paysage urbain parisien.

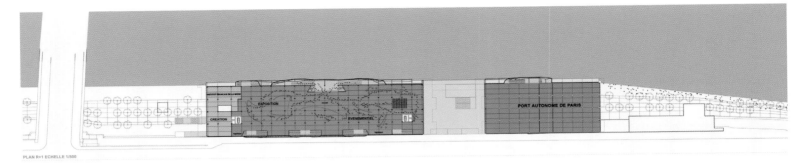

PLAN R+1 ECHELLE 1/500

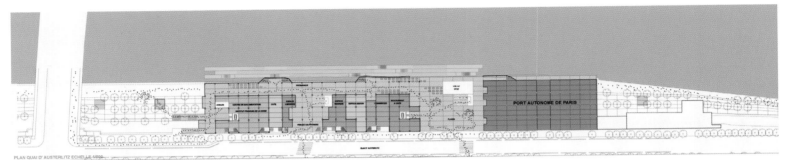

PLAN QUAI D' AUSTERLITZ ECHELLE 1/500

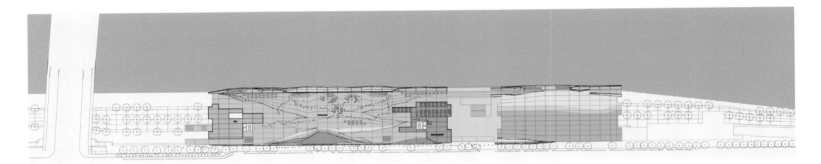

The very contemporary design shows its utilitarian and efficient side in the plans above and the elevation below.

In den Grundrissen und der Ansicht zeigt sich die sehr moderne Gestaltung von ihrer pragmatischen und effizienten Seite.

L'aspect très contemporain de la conception dévoile, dans ces plans et dans l'élévation ci-dessous, ses aspects utilitaires et pragmatiques.

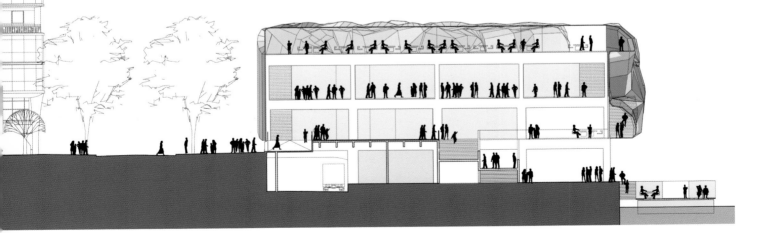

The effort to develop the Seine-front area in the 13th arrondissement of Paris has concerned numerous projects. Here, the otherwise uninviting commercial space has been turned into a real, new "pole of attraction," as the French say for the fashion business.

Nachdem sich schon viele Projekte mit der Sanierung des Gebiets an der Seine im 13. Arrondissement befasst haben, ist es hier tatsächlich gelungen, ein zuvor wenig einladendes kommerzielles Gebäude in einen echten – wie die Franzosen sagen – „pôle d'attractions" der Modeindustrie zu verwandeln.

Le programme de rénovation du front de Seine dans le XIIIe arrondissement de Paris a suscité de nombreux projets. Ici, un espace commercial peu séduisant a été reconverti en pôle d'attraction pour l'univers de la mode.

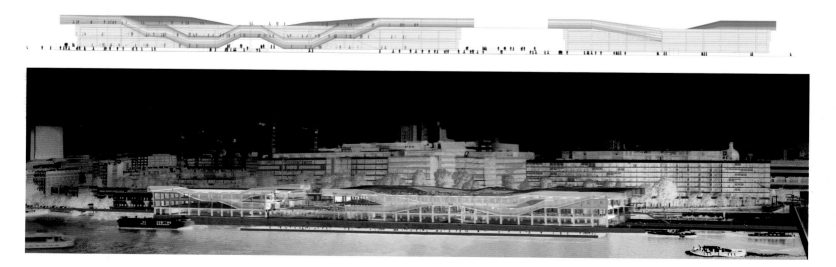

DOCKS DE LYON QUAI RAMBAUD

LYON 2005-09

FLOOR AREA: 12 000 m²
CLIENT: Rhône Saône Development Authority
COST: not disclosed

Located on the Lyon Confluence site where the Austrian architects COOP HIMMELB(L)AU are building the Musée des Confluences (2008), Jakob + Mac Farlane's Quai Rambaud dock project involves a series of pavilions with certain points in common. Geometric structures with "spatial interventions" in the form of cone-like "atrium-patios," which pierce through their outer envelopes, the pavilions have silk-screened patterns on their façades designed with an algorithmic representation of the movement of air and water around the site. The shape of the cones is to be continued beyond the buildings to create "islands" or floating terraces. The "Orange Circle" and "Green Pavilion" are called "boîtes respirantes" or "breathing boxes" by the architects. Jakob + MacFarlane have called on the French artist Bertrand Lavier to create a work in neon for the orange pavilion and on Fabrice Hybert to create a "new type of spa" for the green pavilion. Working with the engineers RFR, Jakob + MacFarlane have suggested rather radical forms and colors that are nonetheless essentially based on box-like buildings.

Jakob+MacFarlanes Projekt für die Docks Quai Rambaud in Lyon liegt am Zusammenfluss von Rhône und Saône, dort, wo auch das Musée des Confluences der österreichischen Architekten COOP HIMMELB(L)AU (2008) gebaut wird. Der Entwurf umfasst eine Abfolge von Pavillons mit bestimmten Gemeinsamkeiten: Es sind geometrische Baukörper mit »räumlichen Interventionen« in Form von kegelartigen Aushöhlungen, die die äußere Gebäudehülle durchstoßen. Die Pavillonfassaden werden im Siebdruckverfahren mit algorithmischen Darstellungen der Luft- und Wasserbewegung in der Umgebung des Grundstücks bedruckt. Die runden Formen sollen auch außerhalb der Gebäude als »Inseln« oder schwimmende Terrassen fortgesetzt werden. Die Architekten bezeichnen den »Circle Orange« und den »Pavillon Vert« als »boîtes respirantes« (atmende Boxen). Jakob+Mac Farlane beauftragten den französischen Künstler Bertrand Lavier mit einer Neonarbeit für den orangefarbenen Pavillon und seinen Kollegen Fabrice Hybert mit einer »neuen Art von Spa« für den grünen Pavillon. In Zusammenarbeit mit den Ingenieuren RFR schlugen die Architekten relativ radikale Formen in leuchtenden Farben vor, die dennoch auf einfachen Kuben basieren.

Sur le site de Lyon Confluence, entre Rhône et Saône et près de l'endroit où s'élèvera le musée des Confluences (2008) des architectes autrichiens COOP HIMMELB(L)AU, le projet de Jakob +MacFarlane pour ces Docks du quai Rambaud comprend une suite de pavillons qui ont certains points communs. Ce sont des structures géométriques à « interventions spatiales » : des patios-atriums en forme de cônes percent leur enveloppe et les pavillons ont des façades ornées de motifs sérigraphiés extraits d'une structure algorithmique créée à partir du mouvement de l'air et de l'eau autour du site. La forme conique se prolonge au-delà des bâtiments, sur le fleuve, pour créer des « îles » ou terrasses flottantes, le « Cercle orange » et le « Pavillon vert », appelés « boîtes respirantes » par les architectes. Jakob + MacFarlane ont fait appel à l'artiste français Bertrand Lavier pour créer une œuvre en néon destinée au pavillon orange et à Fabrice Hyber pour un « nouveau type de spa » dans le Pavillon vert. En collaboration avec les ingénieurs de RFR, les deux architectes proposent ici des formes et des couleurs radicales qui n'en reposent pas moins essentiellement sur le principe de la boîte géométrique.

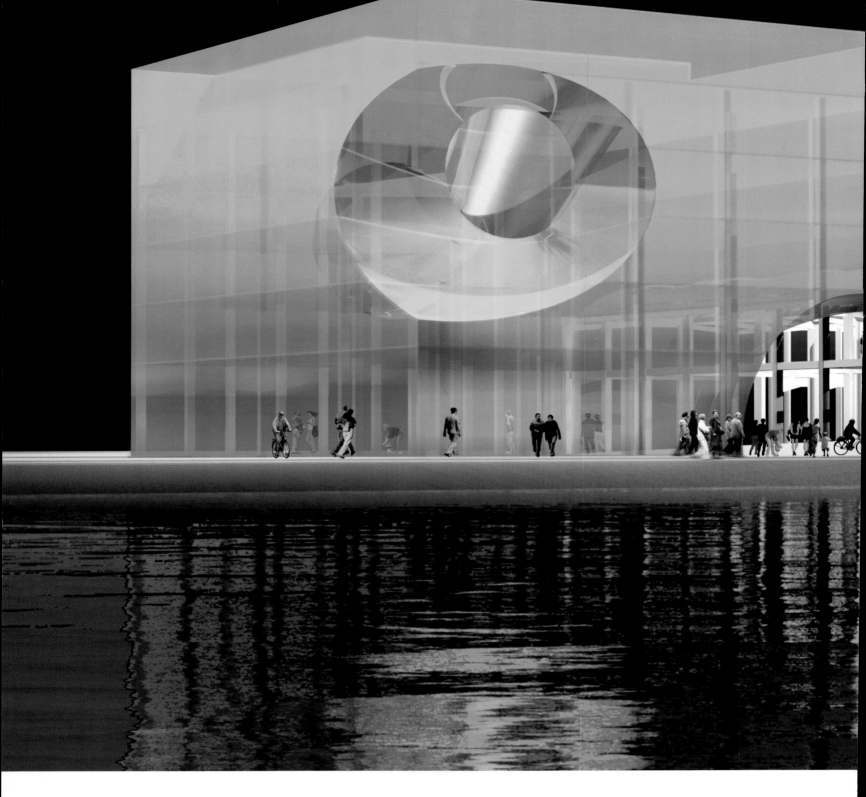

The deep curved cutouts in the building and its situation along the river, together with the bright color scheme, give the Jakob + Mac Farlane project a dynamism that will surely serve to attract the public in the future.

Die tiefen Einschnitte im Gebäude, seine Lage am Fluss sowie kräftige Farben geben dem Projekt von Jacob + und MacFarlanes eine Dynamik, die die Öffentlichkeit in Zukunft ohne Zweifel anziehen wird.

Les découpes franches du bâtiment et la situation au bord du fleuve ainsi que les couleurs vives donnent à ce projet de Jakob + MacFarlane un dynamisme qui saura certaine- ment séduire le public.

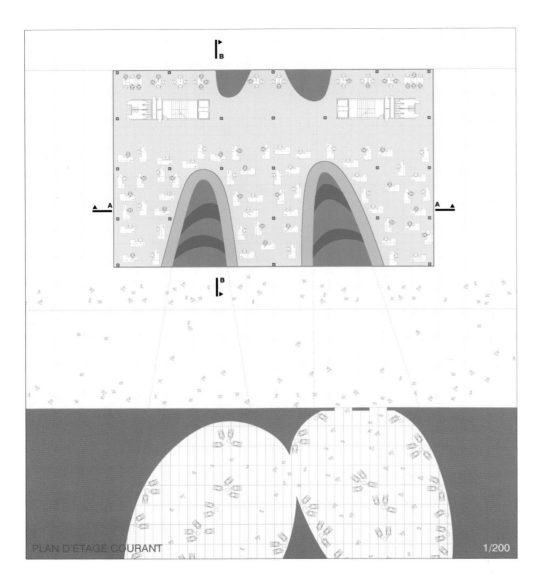

The cutout forms in the building certainly break the monotony of the otherwise modernist block but, beyond that, they penetrate and animate the interior space.

Die Einschnitte in das Gebäude unterbrechen die Monotonie des ansonsten modernistischen Blockes, darüber hinaus durchdringen und beleben sie den Innenraum.

Les découpes rompent avec force la monotonie de ce bloc moderniste, mais ont surtout l'avantage d'animer le volume intérieur et de laisser pénétrer la lumière.

PLAN D'ETAGE COURANT   1/200

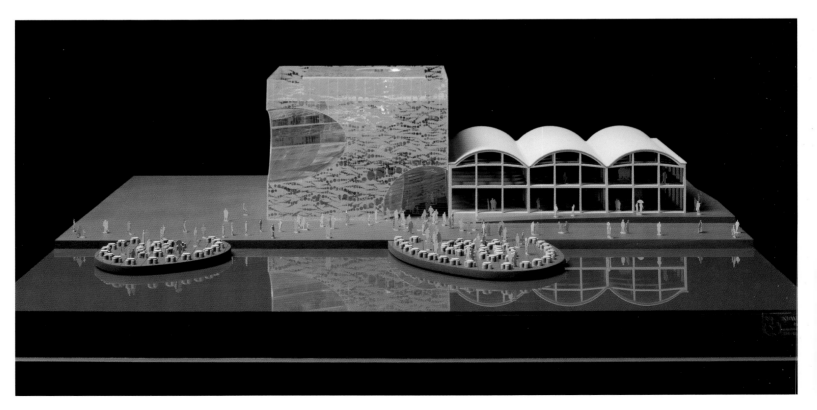

There is something of the irregular curved volumes seen in the earlier Georges Restaurant at the Pompidou Center by the same architects in the bubble-like incursions in the rectilinear form devised for this project.

Die kegelartigen Aushöhlungen in der rechtwinkligen Form erinnern an die von den Architekten für das Restaurant »Georges« im Centre Pompidou entworfenen, unregelmäßig geschwungenen Volumen.

On retrouve dans les « bulles » glissées dans cette forme rectiligne un peu des volumes de courbes libres vus précédemment dans le restaurant Georges du Centre Pompidou.

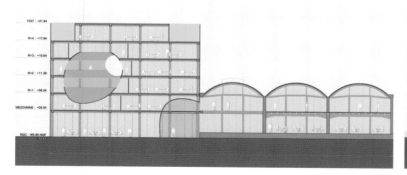

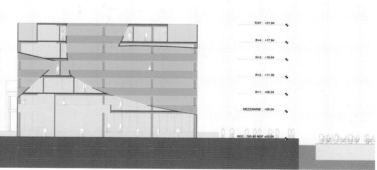

Drawings and a model show how the architects have taken a cubic volume and rendered it surprisingly varied through the use of curved openings that seem to penetrate the volume like the molten forms created by 1960's "lava" lamps.

Die Zeichnungen und das Model zeigen den Kubus, der durch die gewölbten Einbuchtungen eine überraschende Varianz erhält. Ähnlich wie die fließenden Formen in den Lavalampen aus den 1960er Jahren scheinen sie den Baukörper zu durchdringen.

Dessins et maquette montrant comment les architectes ont créé à partir d'un volume cubique une composition étonnement variée à l'aide d'ouvertures incurvées qui semblent la pénétrer et rappellent les formes molles des lampes « lava » des années 1960.

LACATON & VASSAL
206, rue La Fayette
75010 Paris

Tel: +33 1 47 23 49 09
Fax: +33 1 47 23 49 17
e-mail: lacaton.vassal@wanadoo.fr

ANNE LACATON was born in 1955 in Saint-Pardoux la Rivière, France. She received diplomas from the École d'Architecture de Bordeaux (1980) and a DESS degree in Urbanism in Bordeaux in 1984. In 2003–04, she taught for a semester at the École Polytechnique (EPFL) in Lausanne. JEAN-PHILIPPE VASSAL was born in 1954 in Casablanca, Morocco. He received his diploma from the École d'Architecture de Bordeaux (1980) and worked as an architect and city planner in the Niger from 1980 to 1985. He has taught at the École d'Architecture de Bordeaux (1992–99), the Peter Behrens School of Architecture in Düsseldorf (2005) and the École d'Architecture of Versailles (since 2002). Notable projects are the Café of the Architektur Zentrum, Vienna (2001); the renovation of the Palais de Tokyo, a location for contemporary art, Paris (2002); and 14 low-cost residences at the Cité Manifeste in Mulhouse (2005). They have also completed houses in the Dordogne region (1997); Lège Cap Ferret (1998); and Coutras (2000). Current work includes a mixed-use building in Dakar (2006); the Management Sciences building of the Montesquieu University, Bordeaux (2006); the Nantes School of Architecture (2007); social housing in Clermont-Ferrand (2007); and the renovation of the residential Tour Bois-le-Prêtre in Paris (2008).

SOCIAL HOUSING CITE MANIFESTE

ILOT SCHOETTLE, MULHOUSE 2000-05

FLOOR AREA: 14 residences,
2262 m² including garages and winter gardens,
ranging from 175 m² to 102 m² each
CLIENT: SOMCO, Mulhouse
COST: €1.05 million (€75 000 per house)

This welfare housing program includes a total of 61 residences, of which 14 were designed by Lacaton & Vassal. The other architects were Jean Nouvel, Poitevin & Raynaud, Lewis + Block, and Shigeru Ban in collaboration with Jean de Gastines. The site was the former location of a textile plant. For Lacaton & Vassal, known for their minimalist or even rough style, a primary goal was to provide quality housing with the limited budget allotted. They started by creating "a simple, efficient and economical envelope and structure that permitted us to define a maximum volume and floor area, with surprising and contrasted spaces." The ground floor is made of reinforced concrete with a height of more than three meters. The façades are largely glazed and can be opened. A galvanized steel greenhouse with clear polycarbonate panels was placed on this base—partially insulated and heated—with other sections intended for use as winter gardens. Ventilation is achieved by a façade design that allows for half of the surfaces to be opened. Despite this surprising solution, the architects assure that an efficient regulation of temperature and comfort has been achieved. Each of the apartments crosses through the volume and is divided into two levels.

Das Projekt im Bereich sozialer Wohnungsbau umfasst insgesamt 61 Wohnungen; 14 von ihnen wurden von Lacaton & Vassal entworfen. Jean Nouvel, Poitevin & Raynaud, Lewis + Block sowie Shigeru Ban mit Jean de Gastines entwarfen die restlichen Wohnungen für das Grundstück, auf dem sich vorher eine Textilfabrik befand. Ein primäres Anliegen von Lacaton & Vassal, die für ihre minimalistische, bisweilen raue Architektur bekannt sind, war es, qualitativ hochwertige Wohnungen innerhalb des begrenzten Budgets zu realisieren. Sie begannen, indem sie »eine einfache, gut funktionierende und wirtschaftliche Hülle und Tragkonstruktion« entworfen, »die es uns erlaubte, ein maximales Volumen und eine maximale Fläche zu definieren sowie überraschende und kontrastierende Räume vor-

zusehen«. Das Erdgeschoss mit einer Höhe von über 3 m besteht aus Stahlbeton, die Fassaden sind überwiegend verglast und können geöffnet werden. Auf diesem Sockel steht ein Gewächshaus aus verzinktem Stahl mit einer Hülle aus transparenten Polycarbonatpaneelen. Dieser Bereich ist teilweise wärmegedämmt und beheizt, teilweise als Wintergarten konzipiert. Die Belüftung erfolgt über die Fassade, deren Flächen zur Hälfte geöffnet werden können. Die Architekten versichern, dass trotz dieser ungewöhnlichen Lösung eine wirksame Regulierung der Temperatur beziehungsweise der Behaglichkeit gewährleistet ist. Jedes Appartement nimmt die gesamte Tiefe des Gebäudes ein und ist auf zwei Ebenen gegliedert.

Ce programme de logements sociaux sur le site d'une ancienne usine textile comprenait soixante logements dont quarante et un confiés à Lacaton & Vassal, les autres architectes étant Jean Nouvel, Shigeru Ban, Poitevin & Raynaud, Lewis+Block et Shigeru Ban associé à Jean de Gastines. Pour Lacaton & Vassal, connus pour leur style minimaliste voire brut, l'objectif essentiel était d'offrir une réelle qualité de logement dans le cadre d'un budget limité. Ils ont commencé par créer « une enveloppe et une structure simples, efficaces et économiques permettant d'obtenir le maximum de volume et de surface au sol, pour des espaces contrastés et surprenants ». Le rez-de-chaussée en béton armé bénéficie d'une hauteur sous plafond de trois mètres. Une serre en acier galvanisé à vitrage en panneaux de polycarbonate a été posée sur cette base – en partie isolée et chauffée – d'autres sections étant utilisées comme jardins d'hiver. La ventilation est facilitée par la possibilité d'ouvrir à moitié la façade largement vitrée. En dépit de cette surprenante solution, les architectes assurent avoir obtenu un confort et un contrôle de température satisfaisants. Chaque maison est traversante et se répartit sur deux niveaux.

What appears at first glance to be industrial architecture on closer inspection affords pleasant, airy spaces. Given the often gray skies of Mulhouse, the ample openings translate into year-round light, which is more than a traditional configuration would have allowed.

Der auf den ersten Blick vorherrschende Eindruck von Industriearchitektur macht innen angenehmen, luftigen Räumen Platz. Im Vergleich zu einer konventionellen Anordnung führen die großzügigen Öffnungen in der Fassade das ganze Jahr hindurch zu einer besseren Belichtung.

L'aspect industriel de l'architecture se dissout aisément dans les volumes agréables et aérés que l'on peut voir ici. Malgré le ciel souvent gris de Mulhouse, les grandes ouvertures apportent toute l'année un éclairage naturel abondant, ce qu'une solution plus traditionnelle n'aurait pas permis.

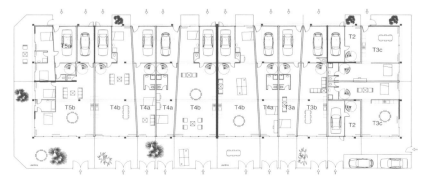

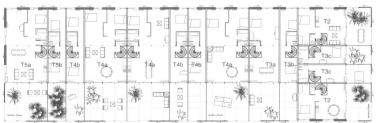

PALAIS DE TOKYO
PARIS
2001 - 02

FLOOR AREA: 7800 m²
CLIENT: Ministère de la Culture–
Délégation aux Arts Plastiques
COST: €4.55 million

This unusual project concerns the renovation of part of the Palais de Tokyo building, erected in Paris in 1937 by the architects Dondel, Aubert, Viart and Dastugue. The eastern wing of the structure has been occupied for some time by the Paris Museum of Modern Art. The west wing belongs to the French government, and was the home of the National Museum of Modern Art until it was moved to the Pompidou Center in 1974. A plan to convert the space into a Museum of Cinema with the architect Franck Hammoutène was abandoned in 1999. The current project envisages the space to be used to display very contemporary art. Measuring almost 9000 m², the spaces of the Palais de Tokyo have ceiling heights varying from four to eight meters. For budgetary reasons, the architects decided to carry out the work necessary for the space to be in conformity with security codes, and to leave the volumes much as they were when they were built. Rough concrete floors and unpainted walls give a temporary or rough quality to the space, which was deemed appropriate to its function as a framework for experimental art.

Das ungewöhnliche Projekt wurde im Rahmen der Renovierung eines Teils des 1937 von den Architekten Dondel, Aubert, Viart und Dastugue erbauten Palais de Tokyo realisiert. Der Ostflügel des Gebäudes wurde einige Zeit vom Pariser Museum für Moderne Kunst eingenommen, während der Westflügel das National-museum für Moderne Kunst beheimatete, das 1974 ins Centre Georges Pompidou verlegt wurde. Den ursprünglichen Plan, das Innere von dem Architekten Franck Hammoutene in ein Filmmuseum umwandeln zu lassen, verwarf man 1999, um die Räumlichkeiten nun für die Präsentation avantgardistischer Kunst zu nutzen.

Die auf fast 9000 m² verteilten Räume des Palais haben Wände mit unterschied-lichen Höhen von vier bis acht Metern. Aus finanziellen Gründen beschlossen die Architekten, das Innere weitgehend so zu belassen, wie es ursprünglich gebaut worden war. Es wurde nur soweit umgebaut, wie es die Sicherheitsvorschriften erforderten. Ungeschliffene Betonböden und Wände im Rauputz verleihen dem Museum einen provisorischen und spröden Charakter, der seiner Funktion als Rahmen für experimentelle Kunst angemessen erscheint.

Étonnant projet que cette rénovation d'une aile du Palais de Tokyo, édifié à Paris en 1937 par les architectes Dondel, Aubert, Viart et Dastugue. L'aile Est abrite le Musée d'art moderne de la ville de Paris, l'aile Ouest, qui appartient à l'État, avait été le siège du Musée national d'art moderne avant qu'il n'emménage au Centre Pompidou en 1974. Son plan de conversion en Cité du cinéma par l'architecte Franck Hammoutène fut abandonné en 1999. Le projet actuel consacre cet espace à la présentation de l'art très contemporain. D'une surface de près de 9000 m², les volumes du Palais de Tokyo bénéficient de hauteurs de plafond de 4 à 8 m. Consi-dérant l'architecture extraordinaire des espaces découverts dans le lieu, et répon-dant à la fois au programme d'installation dans un budget réduit, les architectes ont décidé de simplement réaliser les travaux de mise en sécurité nécessaires et de laisser les volumes tels qu'ils étaient lors de la construction, avant tout aménage-ment. Les sols en béton lissé et les murs non peints confèrent un aspect temporaire, ou brut, à cet espace certainement approprié pour accueillir les témoignages de l'art expérimental.

Stripped down to its bare essentials, the space is ideal for receiving large artworks and a considerable number of visitors.

Der bis auf das Notwendigste reduzierte Ausstellungsraum ist ein idealer Rahmen für großformatige Kunstwerke und zahlreiche Besucher.

Réduit à l'essentiel, le volume convient idéalement aux installations de grandes dimensions et à l'accueil d'un public nombreux.

Given the limited budgets and large floor area, the architects opted for an extremely simple, even industrial approach to materials, ranging from simple concrete floors to standard lighting fixtures, used to augment the ample natural overhead lighting. Bottom right, a view of the interior space of the Palais de Tokyo before the art was brought in.

In Anbetracht des begrenzten Budgets und der großen Nutzfläche entschieden sich die Architekten für den Einsatz äußerst schlichter, industrieller Materialien: ungeschliffene Betonböden und als Ergänzung zur natürlichen Belichtung standardisierte Beleuchtungskörper. Die Ansicht unten rechts zeigt das Interieur, bevor die Kunst Einzug hielt.

Le budget limité et la surface considérable expliquent en partie l'adoption de matériaux simples, quasi industriels, qui vont des sols en béton aux luminaires basiques, Pesquels complètent l'abondant éclairage zénithal naturel. Ci-dessous, à droite : une vue du nouvel espace intérieur du Palais de Tokyo, avant l'installation des œuvres.

MARIN-TROTTIN/ PÉRIPHÉRIQUES ARCHITECTES

PÉRIPHÉRIQUES ARCHITECTES
MARIN+TROTTIN ARCHITECTES
ET AFJUMEAU ARCHITECTE
8, rue Montcalm
75018 Paris

Tel: +33 1 44 92 05 01
Fax: +31 1 44 92 05 14
e-mail: agences@peripheriques-architectes.com
Web: www.peripheriques-architectes.com

Périphériques was created in 1993 by Anne-Françoise Jumeau and Louis Paillard from Jumeau/SoA architects (founded in 1990) and Emmanuelle Marin-Trottin and David Trottin from Marin+Trottin architects (founded in 1992). Each of the two offices continues its independent activities while collaborating on various projects in the fields of architecture, publishing and exhibitions. Anne-Françoise Jumeau was born in 1962, and graduated from Paris-Villemin in 1987. Louis Paillard, born in 1960, left Périphériques in 2003. EMMANUELLE MARIN-TROTTIN, born in 1967, graduated from Paris-La Seine in 1991, while DAVID TROTTIN, born in 1965, graduated from Paris-Villemin in 1990. He taught at the Architecture Schools of Paris-Tolbiac and Paris-Charenton (1996–2000), and at Marne-la-Vallée (2000–2003). Notable projects include: Café Musique, Savigny-le-Temple (2000); Nouveau Casino, Paris (2001); documentation center at the Centre Pompidou, Paris (2002); De La Ville Café, Paris (2003); and Tsumari Belvedere, Japan (2003). In 1999, Périphériques was invited to take part in the Quai Branly Museum competition. Recent work includes: 30 experimental homes in Nantes, Torpedo housing in Saint-Denis, Banlieues Bleues headquarters in Pantin, all completed in 2005; an extension to the Jussieu University in Paris, the Go House in Thionville, and the media-library of a kindergarten in Clamart, all completed in 2006. Périphériques is currently working on the Centre Regional des Musiques Actuelles in Nancy.

GO HOUSE
THIONVILLE
2004 - 06

FLOOR AREA: 300 m²
CLIENT: not disclosed
COST: €600 000 (including land)

Set on a lot near the center of Thionville, this surprising house is surrounded by rather ordinary suburban homes. Local building regulations have encouraged the construction of large residences as compared to the size of the parcels. Périphériques chose to occupy their trapezoidal lot with a form inspired by the shape of the parcel and fill it as much as possible. The architects say that they "conceived the Go House as a strange envelope that resembles a home only in its format." As they point out, the steel frame house with aluminum and glass curtain walls appears to shift back and forth in a way that gives it an impression of lightness. 3-D computer modeling was necessary to determine the actual steel frame design. Floor plans are organized around a central service core and sliding doors permit greater or lesser degrees of privacy for a young couple and their child. The architects have attempted to solve the formal problems posed by their designs before resolving esthetic issues. The unusual appearance of the house lends it a strong presence vis-à-vis the neighborhood. Its upper-floor living room is intended to take advantage of the view and the sunlight, and windows elsewhere intentionally frame views of the surroundings. The clients call the Go House their "UHO" or Unidentified Housing Object, while the architects compare their use of structural materials usually destined for larger buildings to "haute-couture" fashion design.

Das überraschende Haus in der Nähe des Zentrums von Thionville ist von eher gewöhnlichen Vorstadthäusern umgeben. Die örtlichen Bauvorschriften fördern den Bau von im Verhältnis zum Grundstück großen Einfamilienhäusern. Périphériques entschied sich dafür, das trapezförmige Grundstück maximal auszunutzen und mit einer vom Grundstückszuschnitt inspirierten Form zu bebauen. »Das Go House wurde als eine eigenartige Hülle entworfen, die einem Zuhause nur in ihrem ›Format‹ ähnelt«, erläutern die Architekten. Es scheint, darauf weisen sie hin, als ob sich das Haus mit der Tragkonstruktion aus Stahl und den Vorhangfassaden aus Aluminium und Glas vor und zurück bewegen würde, was zum Eindruck der Leichtigkeit führt. Um die tragende Stahlkonstruktion zu planen, mussten 3-D-Computermodelle angefertigt werden. Die Grundrisse sind um einen zentralen Kern mit den Funktionsräumen organisiert. Schiebetüren ermöglichen unter-

schiedliche Grade an Privatsphäre für das junge Paar und sein Kind. Die Architekten versuchten, die formalen Probleme, die sich aus ihren Entwürfen ergeben, zu lösen, bevor sie sich mit ästhetischen Fragen befassten. Das ungewöhnliche Äußere führt zu einer starken Präsenz des Hauses in seiner Umgebung. Das Wohnzimmer im Obergeschoss nutzt die Vorteile des Ausblicks und der Besonnung, die anderen Fenster rahmen bewusst Ausblicke auf die Nachbarschaft. Die Bauherrn nennen das Go House ihr »UHO« (nicht identifiziertes Wohnobjekt), während die Architekten ihre Verwendung der konstruktiven Materialien, die normalerweise für größere Gebäude gedacht sind, mit der Haute Couture in der Mode verglichen.

Construite à proximité du centre de Thionville, cette surprenante résidence est entourée de maisons de banlieue assez ordinaires. La réglementation locale incitait à la construction d'habitations de dimensions importantes par rapport à la taille des parcelles. David Trottin a choisi d'occuper au maximum ce terrain trapézoïdal en y implantant une forme inspirée de celle de la parcelle : « Nous avons conçu la Go House comme une enveloppe étrange qui ne ressemble à une maison que par son format. » Comme les architectes le soulignent, l'ossature en acier à murs rideaux en verre et aluminium semble glisser d'avant en arrière, générant une impression de légèreté. Un logiciel de modélisation 3-D a servi à dessiner très précisément la structure. Les niveaux s'organisent autour d'un noyau central et des portes coulissantes permettent un degré plus ou moins grand d'intimité pour le jeune couple de propriétaires et leur enfant. Périphériques a tenté de résoudre les problèmes formels posés par leur conception avant de s'atteler aux enjeux esthétiques. L'aspect inhabituel de cette maison s'impose fortement par rapport à son voisinage. L'étage du séjour bénéficie de la vue et du soleil et toutes les fenêtres découpent des perspectives sur l'environnement. Les clients parlent de leur maison comme d'un « UHO » ou « Unidentified Housing Object » (Objet logeant non identifié) tandis que les architectes emploient le terme de « haute-couture » pour évoquer leur utilisation de matériaux structurels généralement destinés à des constructions d'échelle plus importante.

The curiously angled walls of the building give the impression that it is capable of motion. Then, too, the materials used give it a translucency that make it altogether contemporary, despite the suburban context in which it was built.

Die ungewöhnliche Geometrie der Wände führt zu dem Eindruck, das Gebäude könne sich bewegen. In seiner vorstädtischen Umgebung wirkt das Gebäude durch die verwendeten transluzenten Materialien sehr modern.

Les murs étonnament inclinés de la construction donnent l'impression qu'elle va se mettre à bouger. Les matériaux lui confèrent une translucidité extrêmement contemporaine, malgré le contexte de banlieue dans lequel il a été édifié.

The house is all the more surprising given the ordinary nature of the neighboring buildings. Large openings are carefully calculated in order to frame a precise view, as is the case with the greenery visible at bottom right.

In Anbetracht der Gewöhnlichkeit der Nachbargebäude überrascht das Haus umso mehr. Große Öffnungen sind sorgfältig angeordnet, um präzise Ausblicke zu rahmen; so auch bei dem Grün unten rechts.

La maison est d'autant plus surprenante que son environnement est très ordinaire. Les grandes ouvertures sont soigneusement calculées pour cadrer des vues précises comme, par exemple visible en bas à droite.

An almost painterly abstraction is confirmed inside the house by the use of bright colors and hovering forms. Openness and light are clearly the themes of this house, which at once ignores its architectural surroundings and affirms its own right to exist in this place.

Innen wird die beinahe malerische Abstraktion des Entwurfs durch die Verwendung kräftiger Farben und schwebender Formen unterstrichen. Offenheit und Licht sind die Themen des Hauses, das seine architektonische Umgebung ignoriert und gleichzeitig auf seinem eigenen Existenzrecht an diesem Ort besteht.

Une abstraction presque picturale se confirme à l'intérieur de la maison grâce aux couleurs vives et aux formes en suspension. L'ouverture et la lumière sont les thèmes affichés de cette maison qui ignore l'environnement architectural et affirme son droit à l'existence à cet endroit.

9

JEAN NOUVEL

ATELIERS JEAN NOUVEL
10, Cité d'Angoulème
75011 Paris

Tel: + 33 1 49 23 83 83
Fax: + 33 1 43 14 81 10
e-mail : info@jeannouvel.fr
Web : www.jeannouvel.com

Born in 1945 in Fumel, France, **JEAN NOUVEL** studied in Bordeaux and then at the Paris École des Beaux-Arts (1964–72). From 1967 to 1970, he was an assistant of Claude Parent and Paul Virilio. In 1970, he created his first office with François Seigneur. His first widely received project was the Institut du Monde Arabe in Paris (1981–87, with Architecture Studio). Other works include his Nemausus housing, Nîmes (1985–87); Lyon Opera House (1986–93); Vinci Conference Center, Tours (1989–93); Euralille Shopping Center, Lille (1991–94); Fondation Cartier, Paris (1991–94); Galeries Lafayette, Berlin (1992–95); and his unbuilt projects for the 400-meter-tall "Tours sans fins," La Défense, Paris (1989); Grand Stade for the 1998 World Cup, Paris (1994); and Tenaga Nasional Tower, Kuala Lumpur (1995). In 2003, Jean Nouvel won a competition sponsored by the Aga Khan Trust for Culture for the design of the waterfront Corniche in Doha, Qatar, and was called on to design the new Guggenheim Museum in Rio de Janeiro. His major completed projects since 2000 are the Music and Conference Center in Lucerne, Switzerland (1998–2000); social housing at the Cité Manifeste, Mulhouse (2001–05); the Quai Branly Museum, Paris (2001–06); the extension of the Reina Sofia Museum, Madrid (1999–2005); the Agbar Tower, Barcelona (1999–2005); and an apartment building in SoHo, New York (2006). Current works include port facilities in Le Havre, France (planned for 2007), and the City Hall, Montpellier (2002–09). Jean Nouvel received the RIBA Gold Medal in 2001.

QUAI BRANLY MUSEUM
PARIS
2001 - 06

FLOOR AREA: 78 000 m²
CLIENT: Etablissement Public
du Musée du quai Branly
COST: 202 million euros

Surely one of the most visible and watched contemporary architecture projects in recent years, this new museum for non-European art is situated on the banks of the Seine near the Eiffel Tower. An earlier project, launched under the presidency of François Mitterrand, had sought to use the same site for an international conference center, but local opposition got the better of the design. Nouvel took the commentary of residents into account, making his rather large building appear to blend into the garden designed by Gilles Clément, and lifting the museum section off the ground, allowing plants (and pedestrians) to walk beneath its bulk. With a glass screen on the riverside that recalls his Fondation Cartier building, the new museum should almost disappear behind large trees. Nouvel was also responsible for the interior museum design and display cases that he intentionally made "too large" so that objects would appear to be liberated from their enclosures. A rooftop area with a broad view of the city and a restaurant complete a facility that includes study and conservation spaces as well as substantial administrative offices.

Sicherlich gehört das neue Museum für außereuropäische Künste am Seineufer, nicht weit vom Eiffelturm, zu den auffälligsten und am genauesten beobachteten Bauprojekten der letzten Jahre. Ein früheres Projekt für dieses Grundstück, ein internationales Konferenzzentrum, das unter der Präsidentschaft von François Mitterrand in Gang gesetzt worden war, scheiterte am Widerstand der Anwohner. Nouvel berücksichtigte die geäußerten Bedenken, fügte das recht große Gebäude sensibel in den von Gilles Clément entworfenen Garten ein und ständerte den Museumsbereich auf, so dass Pflanzen unter dem Baukörper wachsen und Fuß-

gänger hindurchgehen können. Die Glaswand zur Flussseite erinnert an Nouvels Fondation Cartier; das Gebäude wird hinter den großen Bäumen fast verschwinden. Nouvel zeichnet auch für die Ausstellungsarchitektur und -vitrinen verantwortlich. Die Vitrinen sind bewusst »zu groß« konzipiert, um die ausgestellten Objekte aus ihrem Eingeschlossensein zu befreien. Eine Dachterrasse mit weitem Blick über die Stadt und ein Restaurant vervollständigen das Museum, das auch Bereiche für Studien- und Konservierungszwecke sowie die Verwaltung umfasst.

Ce nouveau musée consacré aux arts premiers, sans doute l'une des réalisations d'architecture contemporaine les plus visibles et les plus attendues de ces dernières années, est situé sur la rive gauche de la Seine, non loin de la tour Eiffel. Un projet antérieur lancé sous la présidence de François Mitterrand devait utiliser le même terrain pour un centre international de conférences, mais fut victime de l'opposition des riverains. Nouvel a pris leurs réactions en compte : il a fait en sorte que cette assez vaste construction se fonde dans un jardin conçu par Gilles Clément et a choisi de suspendre la partie muséale au-dessus du sol pour que la végétation et les visiteurs puissent passer sous sa masse. Doté du côté du fleuve d'un écran de verre qui rappelle celui de la Fondation Cartier, le nouveau musée devrait pratiquement disparaître derrière de grands arbres. Nouvel a également été chargé des aménagements intérieurs et des vitrines, qu'il a volontairement dessinées « trop grandes » afin que les objets semblent libérés de leur confinement. Une terrasse sur le toit bénéficiant d'une superbe vue sur la ville et un restaurant complètent ces installations qui comprennent également des locaux pour la conservation et la recherche ainsi que d'importants bureaux.

The museum is located between the quai Branly (to the left in the image above) and the rue de l'Université in the 7th arrondissement of Paris, near the Eiffel Tower. Given the rather complex articulation of the structures visible in the sections below, the museum looks different from every angle.

Das Museum befindet sich in der Nähe des Eiffelturms, zwischen dem Quai Branly (links im Bild oben) und der Rue de l'Université im 7. Pariser Arrondissement. Die Schnitte unten zeigen die komplexe Ausformulierung des Baukörpers – aus jedem Blickwinkel ergeben sich dadurch unterschiedliche Ansichten.

Le musée est situé dans le VIIᵉ arrondissement près de la Tour Eiffel entre le quai Branly (à gauche dans l'image ci-dessus) et la rue de l'Université. Visible dans les coupes ci-dessous, l'articulation assez complexe de ses composantes donne à l'ensemble un aspect très différent selon les angles sous lesquels on le regarde.

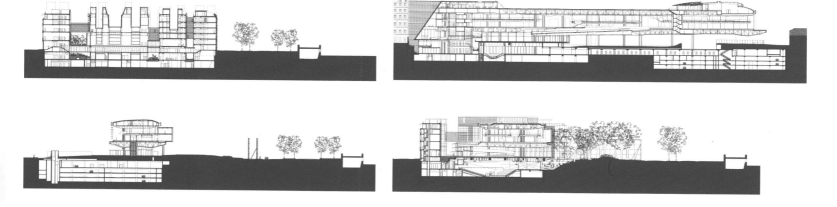

Below, the museum seen from the rue de l'Université. To the left, two early computer perspectives give a very accurate idea of the appearance of the finished structure, including the garden designed by Gilles Clément.

Blick auf das Museum von der Rue de l'Université. Links: Zwei frühe Computerperspektiven vermitteln eine präzise Vorstellung von der Gestaltung des fertigen Gebäudes und dem Garten (Entwurf Gilles Clément).

Le musée vu de la rue de l'Université. À gauche, deux des premières perspectives en image de synthèse qui donnaient déjà une idée très précise de la structure finale, y compris du jardin dessiné par Gilles Clément.

Above, the main exhibition galleries are lifted off the ground on pilotis and the public is free to walk through the gardens from the Seine side to the rue de l'Université side. The configuration of the garden berms is designed, amongst other things, to afford the museum extra protection in case of a surge in the levels of the river.

Die Ausstellungsräume stehen überwiegend auf Pilotis; so wird ein öffentlicher Durchgang von den Seine-Gärten zur Rue de l'Université geschaffen. Die Böschungen dienen unter anderem dazu, das Museum im Fall eines erhöhten Wasserstandes der Seine zu schützen.

Ci-dessus, les galeries d'exposition principales sont surélevées du sol par des pilotis et les visiteurs peuvent passer du côté Seine à la rue de l'Université par le jardin. La configuration des bermes du jardin offre au musée, entre autres, une protection supplémentaire en cas de crue du fleuve.

Plans show how the building arcs through the curved site. Top right, the high glass wall designed by Nouvel for the Seine-side entrance. Bottom right, the vegetal façade created by Patrick Blanc for a museum office block.

Die Grundrisse zeigen, wie sich das Museum der Biegung der Grundstücksform anpasst. Rechts oben: Die hohe Glasfassade mit dem Eingang auf der Seine-Seite. Unten rechts: Die begrünte, von Patrick Blanc entworfene Fassade eines Verwaltungstraktes.

Les plans montrent la manière dont le bâtiment s'insère dans son terrain de forme incurvée. En haut à droite, le haut mur de verre conçu par Nouvel côté Seine. En bas à droite, la façade végétale créée par Patrick Blanc pour l'immeuble des bureaux.

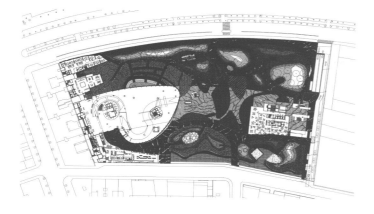

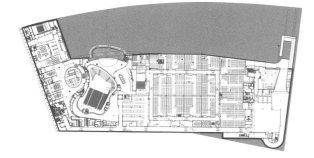

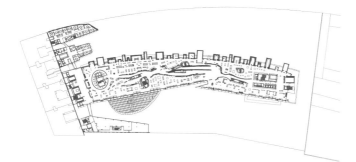

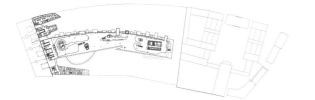

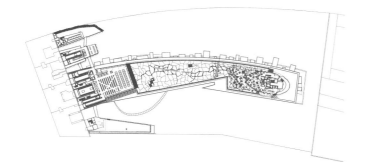

The ground-level spaces of the museum are white (below). A long curved ramp leads up to the darker, more mysterious galleries. Jean Nouvel designed the exhibition cases and curving furniture for the galleries.

Die Räume im Erdgeschoss sind weiß gehalten. Eine lange, geschwungene Rampe führt zu den dunkleren, atmosphärischeren Ausstellungsräumen. Auch die Entwürfe für die Einrichtung der Ausstellungsräume stammen von Jean Nouvel.

Au rez-de-chaussée, les espaces muséaux sont de couleur blanche (ci-dessous). Une longue rampe incurvée monte vers les galeries sombres et mystérieuses. Jean Nouvel a conçu les vitrines d'exposition et le mobilier en courbe des galeries.

SOCIAL HOUSING CITE MANIFESTE ILOT SCHOETTLE, MULHOUSE 2001-05

FLOOR AREA: 11 residences, 1315 m² total
CLIENT: SOMCO, Mulhouse
COST: not disclosed

Each of these residences is different. As the architect describes it, the angles of the walls between apartments give a rhythm to the "whole landscape" of the architecture while translucent peripheral outer walls give an idea of the life inside and out. Woven wood separations give the impression that each resident is in a large garden. Roofs and interior walls are dissociated, and a central void "aids communication between the activities on each level." Orange, rose, blue, green or lilac are employed "to soften the perception of industrial materials and to give a hint of domesticity and rural life," again according to the architect. Trapezoidal gardens, whose form is inspired by the overall configuration of the lot, are intended to counter the orthogonal layout of the larger area of the Cité Manifeste. Although the overall appearance of this apartment complex is rather harsh, indeed very much in the style of Jean Nouvel's other social housing, it offers openness and light, together with a high quality of architecture, not often proposed for such housing projects.

Jede Wohnung unterscheidet sich von der anderen. Wie der Architekt es formuliert, geben die Winkel der Wohnungstrennwände der »Architekturlandschaft« einen Rhythmus. Transluzente Außenwände vermitteln eine Vorstellung des Lebens drinnen und draußen. Geflochtene Trennwände aus Holz erzeugen das Gefühl, sich in einem großen Garten zu befinden. Dächer und Innenwände sind voneinander getrennt und ein zentral angeordneter leerer Raum »unterstützt die Kommunikation bei unterschiedlichen Aktivitäten in jedem Geschoss«. Die Farben Orange, Rosa, Blau, Grün und Lila werden eingesetzt, »um die Wirkung der industriellen Materialien abzumildern und einen Hinweis auf Häuslichkeit und Landleben zu geben«, so noch einmal der Architekt. Trapezförmige Gärten, deren Form von der Gesamtfigur des Grundstücks abgeleitet ist, sollen einen Gegenpol zum orthogonalen System des größeren Gebiets der Cité Manifeste bilden. Obwohl der Gesamteindruck der Wohnanlage eher streng ist und sehr dem Stil von Jean Nouvels anderen Sozialwohnungsbauten entspricht, wurden hier architektonische Qualitäten, Offenheit und eine Belichtung realisiert, die selten bei solchen Wohnprojekten erzielt werden.

Chacune de ces résidences est différente. L'architecte précise que lesdifférents angles des murs mitoyens apportent un rythme au paysage global de la Cité, tandis que les murs périphériques translucides laissent deviner la vie qui se déroule au-dedans comme au dehors. Des séparations de bois tressé font que chaque résident a l'impression de bénéficier d'un grand jardin. Les toits sont dissociés des murs intérieurs et un vide central « facilite la communication entre les activités des différents niveaux ». Les couleurs orange, rose, bleu, vert ou lilas sont utilisées « pour adoucir la perception des matériaux industriels et donner un sentiment de vie à la fois domestique et rurale », toujours selon l'architecte. Les jardins trapézoïdaux dont la forme s'inspire de la configuration d'ensemble du lotissement ont été conçus pour bousculer le plan orthogonal qui est celui de la plus grande partie de la Cité Manifeste. Bien que l'aspect de cet ensemble d'appartements soit assez brut, mais en fait dans l'esprit des autres logements sociaux réalisés par Jean Nouvel, il offre une ouverture, une présence de la lumière et une qualité d'architecture rarement proposées pour ce niveau de loyers.

Behind the metallic exterior are open, high spaces seen in the sections below. Nouvel is well-known for "tough"-looking social housing as he demonstrated with his Nemausus project in Nîmes (1985–87).

Hinter der metallischen Gebäudehülle verbergen sich die offenen hohen Räume, die in den Schnitten unten zu sehen sind. Nouvel ist für seinen »robust« wirkenden sozialen Wohnungsbau, z. B. das Nemausus-Projekt in Nîmes (1985–87), bekannt.

Le caractère métallique de l'architecture r ecouvre les grands volumes ouverts que l'on voit dans les coupes ci-dessous. Nouvel est connu pour ses logements sociaux d'aspect « brut », comme le montre son immeuble « Nemausus », à Nîmes en 1985–87.

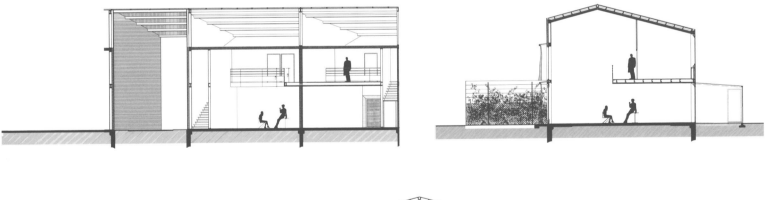

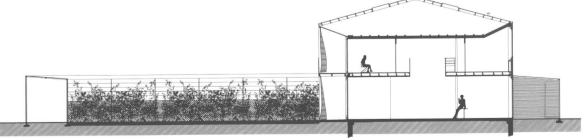

A relatively hard rectilinearity gives way to pleasant living spaces, due in part to the generous glazing and the high ceilings or mezzanine areas, visible in the images below.

Das recht harte rechtwinklige Äußere birgt angenehme Wohnräume, deren Qualität z. T. auf der großzügigen Verglasung sowie den hohen Räumen und Zwischengeschossen beruht.

L'approche relativement dure et rectiligne génère cependant d'agréables espaces de vie, grâce en partie au généreux vitrage et à la hauteur des plafonds et des mezzanines visibles dans les images ci-dessous.

CITY HALL
MONTPELLIER
2003-08

FLOOR AREA: 28 900 m²
CLIENT: City of Montpellier; SERM
(Société d'Équipement de la Région Montpelliéraine)
COST: €52.75 million
ASSOCIATE ARCHITECT: François Fontès

This project involves the construction of a new City Hall, in the context of the second phase of the development of the nine-hectare ZAC Consuls de Mer development area, the first section of which includes housing by Rob Krier. Public spaces, such as a 4.5-hectare park and a 700-place parking lot are part of Nouvel's mission, carried out in this instance in collaboration with François Fontès. The city describes the new structure as a "parallelepiped that is 45 meter high, sitting on a pond and turned toward the Lez River, dominating a 120 m² on the north..." The structure, vertically opened by two patios and horizontally pierced by voids that offer transversal views, will be accompanied by a new park, offices and housing. As he often does, Nouvel has written a descriptive text concerning this project which is under construction. He calls the project "Elle" (She). He writes, "She is in harmony with neighboring architecture... She lives between a large park and the city. She is open and visible like a large transparent open door. Her color is the blue of the sky, of the sea or the coat of arms of Montpellier. Her skin is made of silvery gray wood, while inside, there is another variety of wood, warm, between honey and caramel. She is filled with an interior light. The public spaces open out onto terraces while an interior stairway and panoramic elevators offer views toward the Lez River. Trees, gardens, water, shade, light, filtered images, interference... she is a symbol of hospitality for all residents of Montpellier."

Das Rathaus wird in der zweiten Bebauungsphase des 9 ha großen Entwicklungsgebiets »ZAC Consuls de Mer« realisiert; die erste Phase umfasste u. a. Wohnungen, die von Rob Krier entworfen wurden. In Zusammenarbeit mit François Fontès plant Nouvel auch die öffentlichen Räume – den 4,5 ha großen Park und einen Parkplatz mit 700 Stellplätzen. Von der Stadt wird das neue Rathaus so beschrieben: »... ein durch zwei parallel angeordnete Bauteile strukturiertes 45 m hohes Gebäude über einem Wasserbecken, das sich zum Fluss Lez orientiert und einen nördlich gelegenen 120 m langen Platz dominiert.« Der Bau wird vertikal durch zwei Innenhöfe geöffnet und horizontal von Hohlräumen, die diagonale Durchblicke gewähren, durchstoßen. In seiner Umgebung werden der neue Park, Büro- und Wohngebäude realisiert werden. Nouvel beschreibt das derzeit im Bau befindliche Rathaus in einem Text mit dem Titel »Elle« (Sie): »Sie harmoniert mit der Nachbararchitektur ... Sie lebt zwischen einem großen Park und der Stadt. Sie ist offen und sichtbar wie eine große transparente offene Tür. Sie hat die Farbe des blauen Himmels, des Meeres oder des Wappens von Montpellier. Ihre Haut besteht aus silbergrauem Holz; innen wird es eine andere Holzart geben, warm, zwischen Honig und Karamell. Sie ist erfüllt von einem inneren Licht. Die öffentlichen Räume öffnen sich zu Terrassen, während eine innenliegende Treppe und Panoramaaufzüge Ausblicke auf den Fluss Lez bieten. Bäume, Gärten, Wasser, Schatten, Licht, gefilterte Bilder, Interferenzen ... sie ist ein Symbol der Gastfreundschaft gegenüber allen Einwohnern von Montpellier.«

Ce projet porte sur la construction d'un nouvel hôtel de ville qui sera édifié au cours de la seconde phase de développement de la ZAC Consuls de Mer, dont la première partie comprenait des logements signés Rob Krier. L'intervention de Jean Nouvel, en collaboration avec François Fontès, concerne également quatre hectares et demi de parc public et un parking de sept cents places. La Ville présente la nouvelle construction comme « un parallélépipède de 45 m de haut, au-dessus d'un plan d'eau tourné vers la rivière du Lez, dominant un square de 120 m au nord... La structure, trouée verticalement par deux patios, est percée horizontalement de vides qui offrent des vues transversales et sera accompagnée d'un nouveau parc, de bureaux et de logements. » Comme souvent, Nouvel a rédigé un texte descriptif sur ce projet en construction, intitulé « Elle » : « *Elle* est en harmonie avec l'architecture voisine... elle habite aux confins d'un grand parc et de la ville... Elle se donne à voir comme une grande porte ouverte transparente... Elle affiche la couleur : bleue comme le ciel, comme la mer, comme le blason de Montpellier... Sa peau est faite de bois gris un peu argenté... à l'intérieur c'est une autre essence, plus satinée, chaude, entre miel et caramel... Elle est habitée par une lumière intérieure... Elle offre à ses hôtes des terrasses... à tous son escalier d'honneur... et des ascenseurs panoramiques... Arbres, jardins, terrasses, eau, fraicheur, ombres, lumières, cadrages, filtrages, images, interférences... Elle est un symbole de l'hospitalité pour tous les Montpelliérains. »

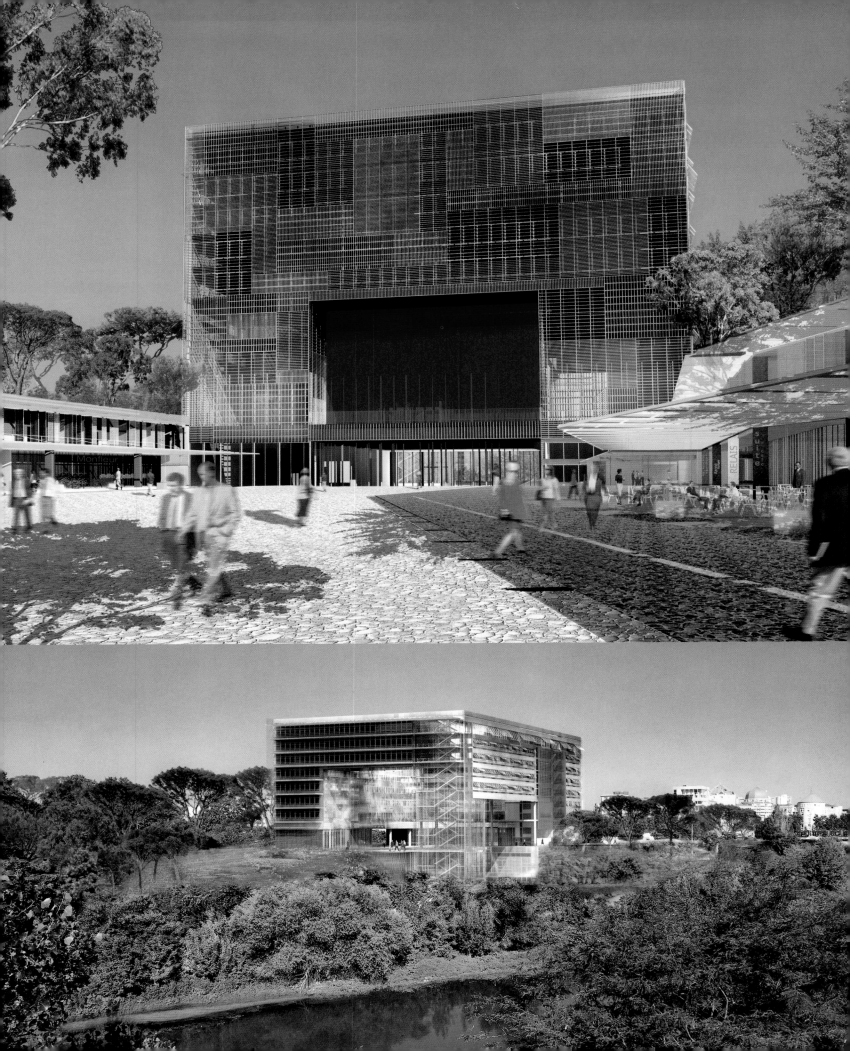

Nouvel's powerful association of water and the dark forms of the building sets him apart from most contemporary architects, who would not dare to make this sort of juxtaposition in the context of a municipal buildling.

Nouvels kraftvolle Anspielung auf Wasser und die dunklen Formen des Gebäudes unterscheiden ihn von den meisten anderen zeitgenössischen Architekten, die diese Art von Nebeneinander im Zusammenhang mit einem öffentlichen Gebäude nicht wagen würden.

L'association de l'eau et des formes sombres du bâtiment distingue Nouvel de la plupart des architectes contemporains qui n'auraient sans doute pas osé ce genre de juxtaposition pour un bâtiment municipal.

Surrounded by greenery, the City Hall stands as a memorable presence. As Nouvel writes: "She reveals herself to be like a large transparent door, open to the light and the park."

Von Grünanlagen umgeben zeigt sich das Rathaus in bemerkenswerter Präsenz. Nouvel schreibt: »Sie gibt sich als großes transparentes Tor, offen zum Licht und zum Park«.

Entourée d'espaces verts, le city hall possède une présence remaquable. Nouvel écrit: « Elle est accueillante. Elle se donne à voir comme une grande porte ouverte transparente sur sa lumière et sur le parc. »

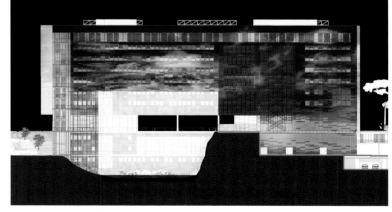
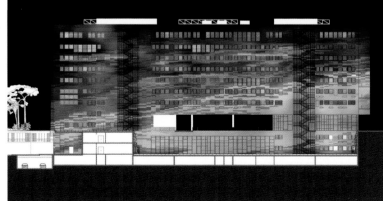

10

DOMINIQUE PERRAULT

**DOMINIQUE PERRAULT
ARCHITECTURE**
26, rue Bruneseau
75629 Paris Cedex 13

Tel: +33 1 44 06 00 00
Fax: +33 1 44 06 00 01
e-mail: dominique.perrault
@perraultarchitecte.com
Web: www.perraultarchitecte.com

DOMINIQUE PERRAULT was born in 1953 in Clermont-Ferrand. He studied in Paris and received his diploma as an architect from the École des Beaux-Arts in 1978. He received a further degree in urbanism at the École Nationale des Ponts et Chaussées in 1979, as well as a Master's degree in History at the EHESS in 1980. He founded his own firm in 1981 in Paris. His first well publicized works were the Engineering School (ESIEE), Marne-la-Vallée (1984–87); the Hôtel industriel Berlier, Paris (1986–90); the Applix factory, Cellier-sur-Loire (1991–99); and the Town Hall / Hybrid Hotel, Innsbruck, Austria (2000-02). His major projects include the French National Library in Paris (1989-95) and the Olympic Velodrome, Swimming and Diving Pool, Berlin (1992–99). Recent buildings include the Media Library, Vénissieux (1997–2001); the design of several supermarkets for the M-Preis chain in Austria (1999–2003); the refurbishment of the Piazza Gramsci, Cinisello Balsamo, Milan (1999-2004); and the master plan for the Donau City, Vienna (2002–03). Current projects include: a redesign of the urban waterfront "Las Teresitas" (2000-06) and the construction of a 5-star hotel (2000-08), both in Tenerife, Canary Islands; the Habitat Sky Tower, Barcelona (2002-07); the Olympic Tennis Center, Madrid (2002-07); the new Mariinsky Theater, Saint-Petersburg (2003-09); the Ewha Women's University, Seoul (2004–07); the Sky Tower, Vienna (2004-08); the redevelopment of the banks of the Manzanares, Madrid (2005-08); and an extension of the Court of Justice of the European Community, Luxembourg (2008).

MEDIA LIBRARY
VENISSIEUX
1999 - 2001

FLOOR AREA: 5230 m²
CLIENT: City of Vénissieux
COST: €6.05 million

The winner of a 1997 public competition, Dominique Perrault began, with this project, to break out of a certain professional isolation that followed his very visible National Library in Paris. "We imagined we were building a glass box on a public square. Inside the box all of the functions of the project are located on the same level and surrounded by a peristyle," says Dominique Perrault. Actually, the box has façades made of a sandwich of perforated metal and glass. Offices are set in another box on the roof of the structure. Natural overhead lighting is provided, giving a more luminous space than might be expected of the exterior of this mediatheque for a community of 56 000 people located to the south of Lyon. Just as Mantes-la-Jolie is best known for the Val Fourré social housing zone, Vénissieux has a similarly difficult area, known as the Cité des Minguettes. It may not be an accident that despite its description as an open place, the Vénissieux Media Library has something of a closed, metallic appearance. Having designed the furniture as well, Perrault uses them to divide the interior space while maintaining the overall appearance of openness that he seeks. The winner of one of the World Architecture ARUP Awards for the "best buildings of 2001," Perrault's building was cited by the jury for its social commitment and specially developed façades. "Perfectly detailed" and "really ingenious" were among the judges's comments.

1997 gewann Dominique Perrault den offenen Wettbewerb für die Mediathek in Vénissieux. Mit ihr gelang es ihm, aus einer gewissen Isolierung innerhalb der Architektenschaft auszubrechen, die auf den sehr auffälligen Bau der Bibliothèque Nationale de France in Paris folgte. »Wir stellten uns vor, wir würden auf einem öffentlichen Platz eine Glaskiste bauen. In dieser Kiste befinden sich, umgeben von einem Peristyl, alle Funktionen auf einer Ebene«, erläutert Perrault. Die Fassaden der Box wurden letztlich nicht aus Glas, sondern aus Sandwichpaneelen aus perforiertem Metall und Glas gefertigt. Auf dem Dach des Gebäudes befinden sich in einer weiteren Box die Büros. Die Mediathek wird über Oberlichter natürlich belichtet, was sie heller macht, als man ihrer äußeren Erscheinung nach

vermuten könnte. Vénissieux liegt südlich von Lyon und hat 56 000 Einwohner. So wie Mantes-la-Jolie für seinen sozialen Wohnungsbau im Fourré-Tal steht, gibt es in Vénissieux ein ähnliches Problemgebiet, Cité des Minguettes. Vielleicht ist es kein Zufall, dass die Mediathek trotz ihrer Charakterisierung als ein offener Ort ein geschlossenes, metallisches Äußeres zeigt. Mit der Möblierung, die Perrault ebenfalls entwarf, wird der Innenraum gegliedert und behält gleichzeitig die vom Architekten gewollte Offenheit. Die Mediathek wurde als eins der »besten Gebäude 2001« mit einem World Architecture ARUP Award ausgezeichnet; die Jury honorierte das soziale Engagement und die speziell entwickelte Fassade. »Perfekt im Detail« und »wirklich genial« kommentierte die Jury.

C'est grâce à cette réalisation remportée en 1997 à l'issue d'un concours que Dominique Perrault a commencé à rompre le relatif isolement qui avait suivi sa très remarquée Bibliothèque nationale à Paris. « Nous avons imaginé de construire une boîte de verre sur une place publique. À l'intérieur, toutes les fonctions sont regroupées sur un même niveau entouré d'un péristyle », explique l'architecte. Concrètement, la « boîte » possède des façades en sandwich de verre et de métal perforé. Les bureaux se trouvent dans une seconde « boîte » implantée sur le toit. L'éclairage zénithal génère un espace plus lumineux que ce que laisse présager l'aspect extérieur de cette médiathèque réalisée pour une commune de 56 000 habitants de la banlieue sud de Lyon, connue pour son quartier difficile, la Cité des Minguettes. Ce n'est peut-être pas un hasard si l'édifice a été doté de cette apparence métallique et fermée. Perrault s'est servi du mobilier, qu'il a également conçu, pour diviser l'espace intérieur tout en conservant l'aspect ouvert recherché. Cette réalisation a remporté le World Architecture ARUP Award de « meilleur bâtiment de l'année 2001 » pour ses façades spécifiquement mises au point pour le projet, sa valeur sociale, la « qualité de sa réalisation » et son caractère « réellement ingénieux ».

Perrault has often played with the contrast of closed, defensive surfaces and nature, as he did with the French National Library in Paris. Here transparency and opacity alternate to create an affirmed identity.

Perrault hat oft mit dem Kontrast von geschlossenen, defensiv wirkenden Oberflächen und Elementen aus der Natur gespielt. Die Bibliothèque Nationale de France ist dafür in vielerlei Hinsicht ein Beispiel. Bei diesem Projekt wechseln sich Transparenz und Opazität ab, um dem Gebäude eine starke Identität zu geben.

Perrault a souvent joué sur le contraste entre des surfaces fermées, quasi défensives, et une mise en scène de la nature, par exemple pour la Bibliothèque nationale de France à Paris. Ici, la transparence et l'opacité alternent pour donner naissance à une identité forte.

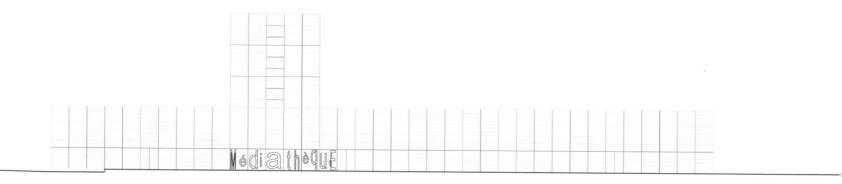

As with the National Library, Perrault demonstrates a clear capacity to harmonize interior and exterior design. The rather closed appearance of the building's exterior gives way to a moderate translucency inside that eschews evoking claustrophobic feelings in the visitor.

Wie bei der Bibliothèque Nationale de France beweist Perrault hier seine Fähigkeit, die Gestaltung der Innenräume und der äußeren Hülle in Einklang zu bringen. Die eher geschlossene Außenwirkung des Gebäudes macht innen einer gemäßigten Transluzenz Platz, die kein Gefühl von Eingeschlossensein aufkommen lässt.

Comme pour la Bibliothèque nationale, Perrault montre ici sa capacité à harmoniser la conception de l'intérieur et celle de l'extérieur. L'aspect extérieur assez fermé du bâtiment fait place, à l'intérieur, à des effets de translucidité contrôlés qui gomment tout sentiment claustrophobique.

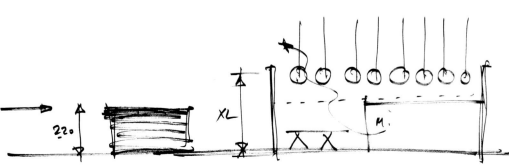

NAUTICAL CENTER
MANTES-LA-JOLIE
2005

FLOOR AREA: 4977 m²
CLIENT: Communauté d'Agglomération
de Mantes en Yvelines
COST: €11.5 million

Located 53 kilometers to the west of Paris, Mantes-la-Jolie and its Val Fourré area have long been rather notorious, despite several reconstruction programs seeking to improve the living conditions of the local population. Near Val Fourré, at the edge of the rowing basin of Mantes-la-Jolie, Dominique Perrault has designed a "nautical center" that combines a group of swimming pools and facilities for the basin. Perrault says, "Our urban and architectural goal was to propose a building that is radically different from the existing environment, which is made up largely of large-scale social housing." Working with the landscape architect Michel Desvignes, Perrault wanted to create a "joyful and luminous" space made up of "curves and counter-curves." Divided into two buildings corresponding to the two functions, the complex has one wooden "hangar"-type structure for the rowing basin and a "water space" in the shape of waves for the swimming pools. Rather than creating something like an "Olympic swimming facility," the architect intentionally encourages togetherness and relaxation. Making use of the natural setting at the edge of the Seine, together with new garden spaces, the complex aims to improve the living conditions of the residents of Mantes-la-Jolie.

Mantes-la-Jolie, 53 km westlich von Paris gelegen, und das Fourré-Tal genießen schon lange einen zweifelhaften Ruf, der sich auch durch mehrere Sanierungsprogramme, mit denen die Wohnbedingungen für die benachteiligte Anwohnerschaft verbessert werden sollten, nicht verbessert hat. In der Nähe des Fourré-Tals, am Rand des Ruderbeckens von Mantes-la-Jolie, befindet sich der von Dominique Perrault entworfene Pôle Nautique, der sowohl mehrere Schwimmbassins als auch die Einrichtungen für das Ruderbecken umfasst. Perrault sagt: »Unser städtebauliches und architektonisches Ziel war es, ein Gebäude vorzuschlagen, das sich radikal von dem vorhandenen Umfeld unterscheidet, das im Wesentlichen vom sozialen Wohnungsbau in großem Maßstab geprägt wird.« In Zusammenarbeit mit dem Landschaftsarchitekten Michel Desvignes wollte Perrault einen »fröhlichen Raum voller Licht« schaffen, der sich aus »Bögen und Gegenbögen« zusammensetzt. Die Anlage besteht entsprechend ihren beiden Funktionen aus zwei Gebäuden. Für die Einrichtungen der Ruderanlage gibt es ein Gebäude mit einer hangarartigen Holzkonstruktion, für die Schwimmbecken einen wellenförmigen »Wasserraum«. Perrault ging es weniger darum, eine olympische Schwimmanlage zu bauen, vielmehr suchte er bewusst nach Möglichkeiten, das gemeinsame Erlebnis und die Entspannung zu unterstützen. Durch seine Lage am Seine-Ufer und im Zusammenhang mit den neuen Gärten soll der Komplex endlich das Wohnumfeld der Bewohner von Mantes-la-Jolie verbessern.

Située à cinquante-trois kilomètres à l'ouest de Paris, Mantes-la-Jolie et son quartier du Val Fourré se sont rendus tristement célèbres en raison de leurs problèmes sociaux, malgré plusieurs programmes de réhabilitation destinés à améliorer les conditions d'existence des populations défavorisées qui y habitent. Près du Val Fourré et du bassin de loisirs municipal, Dominique Perrault a conçu ce Centre nautique qui réunit plusieurs piscines et les installations sportives du bassin. Pour l'architecte, « [notre] objectif urbain et architectural était de proposer un bâtiment radicalement différent de l'environnement existant, lequel est composé surtout de grands ensembles de logements sociaux ». En collaboration avec l'architecte-paysagiste Michel Desvignes, Perrault a voulu créer un espace « joyeux et lumineux », tout en « courbes et contre-courbes ». Le Centre se répartit en deux bâtiments correspondant à ses deux fonctions : une construction de type hangar en bois pour le bassin de loisirs et un « espace d'eau » en forme de vague pour les piscines. Plutôt que de travailler dans un esprit de piscine olympique, l'architecte a cherché à encourager résolument l'échange et la détente. À partir de ce cadre naturel en bordure de Seine et de nouveaux aménagements paysagers, ces installations ont pour but de contribuer à améliorer les conditions de vie des Mantois.

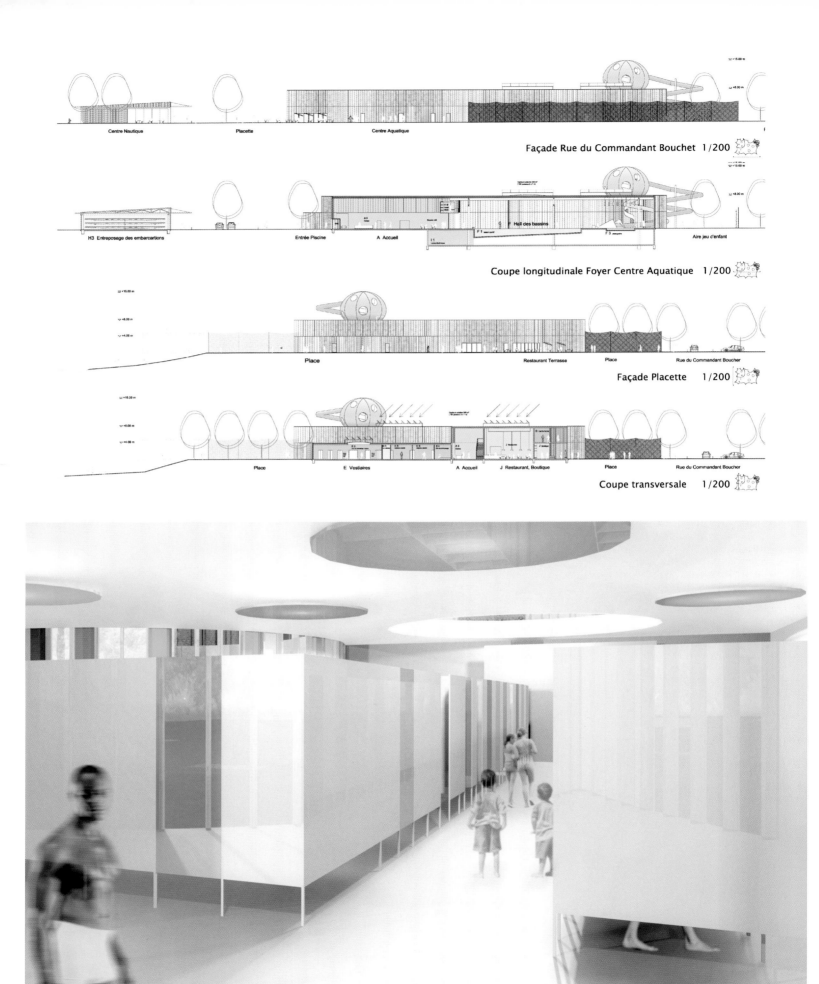

Centre Nautique   Placette   Centre Aquatique

Façade Rue du Commandant Bouchet   1/200

H3 Entreposage des embarcations   Entrée Piscine   A Accueil   F Hall des bassins   Aire jeu d'enfant

Coupe longitudinale Foyer Centre Aquatique   1/200

Place   Restaurant Terrasse   Place   Rue du Commandant Boucher

Façade Placette   1/200

Place   E Vestiaires   A Accueil   J Restaurant, Boutique   Place   Rue du Commandant Boucher

Coupe transversale   1/200

Given the rather difficult urban context of this project, the architect has responded with colors and forms that might be considered atypical of his often harder materials and tones. Curves and openings alternate with the more rectilinear outer perimeter of the design.

In Anbetracht des eher schwierigen städtebaulichen Kontextes, mit dem er es zu tun hatte, antwortete der Architekt mit Farben und Formen, die nicht unbedingt typisch für ihn sind – sonst verwendet er eher »robustere« Materialien und kräftigere Farbtöne. Kurven und Öffnungen kontrastieren mit der rechtwinkligen äußeren Form des Gebäudes.

Face au contexte urbain assez difficile dans lequel il était appelé à intervenir, l'architecte a répondu par des formes et des couleurs assez atypiques par rapport à ses choix habituels, généralement plus radicaux quant aux matériaux et aux teintes. Les courbes et les ouvertures alternent avec les lignes extérieures plus rectilignes du projet.

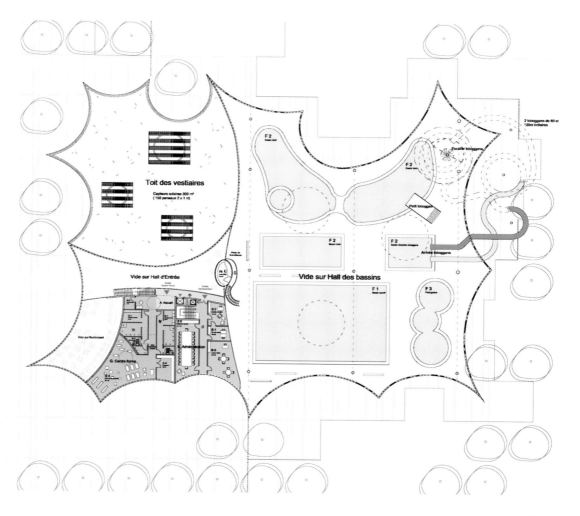

11

CHRISTIAN DE PORTZAMPARC

ATELIER CHRISTIAN
DE PORTZAMPARC
architecte urbaniste
1, rue de l'Aude
75014 Paris

Tel: +33 1 40 64 80 00
Fax: +33 1 43 27 74 79
e-mail:
studio@chdeportzamparc.com
Web: www.chdeportzamparc.com

CHRISTIAN DE PORTZAMPARC was born in Casablanca, Morocco, in 1944. He studied at the École des Beaux-Arts, Paris (1962–69), and founded his own firm in 1980. Built projects include his Water Tower, Marne-la-Vallée (1971–74); Hautes Formes public housing, Paris (1975–79); Cité de la Musique, Paris (1985–95); extension for the Bourdelle Museum, Paris (1988–92); Housing, Nexus World, Fukuoka, Japan (1989–92); a housing complex at the ZAC Bercy, Paris (1991–94); and Crédit Lyonnais Tower, Euralille, Lille (1992–95), built over the Lille-Europe railway station in Lille. Other works include a courthouse for Grasse in the south of France (1993–97); the LVMH Tower on 57th Street, New York (1996–99); an addition to the Palais des Congrès, Paris (1996–99); and the Espace Lumière office building, Boulogne-Billancourt (1996–99). Recently completed works are the French Embassy, Berlin (1997–2003); the Philharmonic concert hall, Luxembourg (1997–2005); the headquarters of the daily Le Monde, Paris (2001–04); and the Champs Libres museum and bookshop, Rennes (2002–06). His current projects include the masterplan for the Massena neighborhood, Paris (1995–2007); the Rio Concert Hall, Rio de Janeiro (2002–07); and an apartment building on Park Avenue South, New York (2002–09). Christian de Portzamparc was awarded the 1994 Pritzker Prize.

LE MONDE HEADQUARTERS
PARIS
2001 - 04

FLOOR AREA: 18 118 m²
CLIENT: Le Monde
COST: €26.67 million

Completed in December 2004, this project involved the restructuring of the offices of the prestigious French daily newspaper *Le Monde*. Located on the boulevard Auguste Blanqui in the 13th arrondissement of Paris, the project involved offices, a 148-seat auditorium, a cafeteria, restaurant, inner garden and parking space, and was completed in 18 months. The most visible feature of the restructuring is the new façade made with Saint Gobain glass and Reynobond aluminum composite panels. As Portzamparc says, "From the outset, it was obvious that this anonymous 1970s building had to be given a presence on the boulevard while we undertook the renovation and transformation of the office areas. The work done is at once technical, functional and esthetic." Portzamparc sliced part of the top of the old building off in order to permit the structure no longer to be considered a "tall building" in terms of zoning laws. The main section of the building was enlarged, to compensate for the reduction in height. A bright central atrium and other openings underline the architect's desire for transparency. A double-skin façade with silk-screened glass representing the front page of the daily renders the identity of the building perfectly clear. Portzamparc's wife, Elizabeth, participated in the interior design of the building for the winter garden, cafeteria and "relaxation" area.

Das Projekt, fertig gestellt im Dezember 2004, umfasst die Neuorganisation der Büros der angesehenen französischen Tageszeitung *Le Monde* am Boulevard Auguste Blanqui im 13. Arrondissement von Paris. Außerdem wurden weitere Büros, ein Saal mit 148 Plätzen, eine Cafeteria, ein Restaurant, ein Hofgarten sowie Parkplätze geschaffen; die Bauarbeiten dauerten 18 Monate. Das auffälligste Element des Umbaus ist die neue Fassade, die aus Glas der Firma Saint Gobain und aus Kompositpaneelen aus Aluminium der Firma Reynobond besteht. Portzamparc erläutert: »Von Beginn an war klar, dass – über die Instandsetzung und Umwandlung der Bürobereiche hinaus – das anonyme Gebäude aus den 1970er Jahren zum Boulevard einen neuen Auftritt brauchte. Die Maßnahmen, die wir ergriffen, sind gleichzeitig technischer, funktionaler und ästhetischer Art.« Portzamparc reduzierte die Höhe des alten Gebäudes teilweise, wodurch es nicht mehr als Hochhaus gilt und andere Abstandsregeln gelten. Um den Raumverlust durch die verringerte Höhe zu kompensieren, wurde die Tiefe in einem wesentlichen Teil des Hauses vergrößert. Ein helles, zentrales Atrium und Öffnungen in der Fassade unterstreichen den Wunsch des Architekten nach Transparenz. Eine zweischalige Fassade mit einer äußeren Glasebene, auf die eine Titelseite der Zeitung im Siebdruckverfahren aufgebracht wurde, gibt die Identität des Gebäudes sehr deutlich zu erkennen. An der Innenraumgestaltung der Zentrale war Portzamparcs Ehefrau Elizabeth beteiligt.

Achevé en décembre 2004, ce projet a consisté en la restructuration d'un immeuble de bureaux, boulevard Auguste Blanqui dans le XIIIe arrondissement de Paris, pour le prestigieux quotidien français *Le Monde*. Outre les bureaux de la rédaction et de l'administration, le programme comprenait une salle de conférences de cent quarante-huit places, une cafétéria, un restaurant, un jardin intérieur et des parkings. Il a été réalisé en dix-huit mois. L'élément le plus visible de la restructuration est la façade en verre Saint-Gobain et panneaux de composite d'aluminium Reynobond. Comme l'explique Christian de Portzamparc, « dès le départ, il était évident que cet immeuble anonyme des années 1970 devait imposer sa présence sur le boulevard... Le travail réalisé est à la fois technique, fonctionnel et esthétique. » L'architecte a coupé une partie du sommet de la construction qui, ainsi, ne pouvait plus être classée parmi les immeubles de grande hauteur. La partie principale a été élargie pour compenser la réduction de hauteur. Un vaste et lumineux atrium central et d'autres ouvertures expriment le désir de transparence manifesté dans l'ensemble du projet. Une façade à double-peau en verre sérigraphié représentant la première page du journal affiche clairement l'identité de l'immeuble. Elizabeth de Portzamparc, épouse de l'architecte, a participé à l'aménagement du jardin d'hiver, de la cafétéria et des espaces de détente.

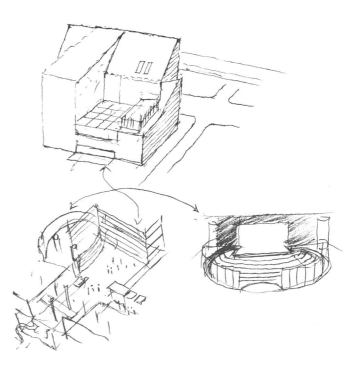

By adding a layer to the front of the building to reproduce an over-sized version of the front page of the famous French daily, Portzamparc has both modernized the architecture and projects an image of the daily to passers-by and users of the building.

Indem er vor die straßenseitige Fassade eine weitere Ebene stellte und auf ihr eine überdimensionale Titelseite der bekannten französischen Tageszeitung projezierte, modernisiert Portzamparc die Architektur des bestehenden Gebäudes und schafft ein Bild, dem sich weder Nutzer noch Passanten entziehen können.

En doublant la façade de l'immeuble d'une immense reproduction sur verre de la première page du fameux quotidien, Portzamparc a réussi à la fois à moderniser l'architecture et à en graver une image frappante tant dans l'esprit des passants que dans celui des usagers de l'immeuble.

In these interior views, it appears that Portzamparc has somewhat tempered his taste for the "lyrical" modernism that he is best known for. Horizontal banding of both the glazing and the interior cladding of the floors above ground level create a continuity in the space.

Bei den Innenräumen scheint es, als ob Portzamparc seine Vorliebe für einen »lyrischen« Modernismus, für die er bekannt ist, ein wenig gezähmt hätte. Horizontale Bänder aus Glas und die bandartige Innenverkleidung der Ebenen über dem Erdgeschoss schaffen eine räumliche Kontinuität.

D'après ces vues intérieures, Portzamparc semble avoir quelque peu tempéré le goût du modernisme « lyrique » qui l'a rendu célèbre. Les bandes horizontales des vitrages et des habillages intérieurs des différents niveaux créent une continuité dans l'espace.

RENNES CULTURAL CENTER - LES CHAMPS LIBRES

RENNES 2002·06

FLOOR AREA: 26 846 m²
CLIENT: Rennes Metropole
COST: €55 million

This complex was designed to include three institutions, and was the result of a 1993 competition. The Municipal Library occupies five levels. The Science Space includes a 100-seat planetarium, temporary and permanent exhibition space and a children's area. The third element in the composition is the Museum of Brittany, conceived around the theme "Brittany is a universe." Temporary exhibition spaces for the museum are located on the ground and first floors. The museum design was handled by Elizabeth de Portzamparc. A cafeteria, boutique, museum workshops, administrative and curatorial offices, and a 460-seat auditorium complete Champs Libres. As Portzamparc says, from the outset, he was determined to give each of the three institutions a separate, legible identity despite the unified complex. Located on the site of a former bus terminal, and near the Charles de Gaulle square, which had essentially become a parking lot, the site required nothing less than a "transformation of the urban situation," according to the architect. He gave the museum a horizontal form "floating above the ground floor," and created two vertical volumes that cross through this flat plate. The Science Space was given a conical form with the spherical planetarium at the top. The library "rises toward the sky." A cone and an inverted pyramid are the basic shapes involved. Portzamparc designed the concrete cladding panels in collaboration with the sculptor Martin Wallace. Other materials include Lanhénin granite and other locally mined stones, firmly anchoring this modern structure in the earth of Brittany.

Der Komplex basiert auf einem Wettbewerbsentwurf von 1993. Er umfasst drei Einrichtungen: die Städtische Bibliothek, die auf fünf Ebenen untergebracht ist, den Wissenschaftsbereich, der aus einem Planetarium mit 100 Sitzen, Räumen für wechselnde und ständige Ausstellungen und einem Bereich für Kinder besteht, sowie das Musée de Bretagne, das unter dem Motto »Die Bretagne – ein Universum« steht. Die Räume für wechselnde Ausstellungen nehmen das Erd- und erste Obergeschoss ein. Die Gestaltung des Museums geht auf Elizabeth de Portzamparc zurück. Ergänzt wird Champs Libres durch eine Cafeteria, eine Boutique, Museumswerkstätten und Büros für die Verwaltung und Kuratoren. Portzamparc sagt, dass er jeder der drei Institutionen eine eigenständige, lesbare Identität geben wollte, obwohl es sich um einen Gesamtkomplex handelt. Das Grundstück in der Nähe der Place Charles de Gaulle, auf dem sich früher ein Busbahnhof befand, diente anschließend vorwiegend als Parkplatz. Es bedurfte, so der Architekt, nicht weniger als einer »Transformation der städtebaulichen Situation«. Er gab dem Museum eine horizontale Form, »die über dem Erdboden schwebt«. Zwei vertikale Baukörper durchstoßen die flache Scheibe. Der Forschungsbereich ist kegelförmig und nach oben durch das gewölbte Planetarium abgeschlossen. Die Bücherei »wächst gen Himmel« – ein Kegel und eine umgedrehte Pyramide sind hier die Grundformen. Die Betontafeln der Außenverkleidung entwickelte Portzamparc in Zusammenarbeit mit dem Bildhauer Martin Wallace. Weitere verwendete Materialien sind Granit aus Lanhénin sowie andere Natursteine aus der Region, die die Verbindung des modernen Gebäudes mit der Bretagne unterstreichen.

Cet ensemble qui regroupe trois institutions culturelles avait fait l'objet d'un concours en 1993. La Bibliothèque municipale est logée sur cinq niveaux déclinant divers thèmes. L'Espace des sciences comprend un planétarium de cent places, des salles d'expositions permanentes et temporaires et une zone pour les enfants. Le troisième élément est le Musée de Bretagne, conçu autour du thème « La Bretagne est un univers ». Les espaces d'expositions temporaires du musée sont logés au rez-de-chaussée et au premier étage. La muséographie est signée Elizabeth de Portzamparc. Une cafétéria, une boutique, les ateliers du musée, les bureaux de l'administration et de la conservation et un auditorium de quatre cent soixante places complètent l'ensemble. C. de Portzamparc était déterminé dès le départ à donner à chacune des trois institutions une identité autonome et lisible, même dans le cadre d'un complexe unificateur. Situé sur une ancienne gare routière et près de la place Charles-de-Gaulle qui s'était peu à peu muée en parking, le site ne réclamait pas moins qu'une « transformation de la situation urbaine ». L'architecte a voulu cette forme horizontale « flottant juste au-dessus du sol » et a créé deux volumes verticaux qui traversent cette dalle. L'Espace des sciences occupe une forme conique au sommet de laquelle se trouve le planétarium. Quant à la bibliothèque en pyramide inversée, elle « s'élève vers le ciel ». Portzamparc a dessiné les panneaux d'habillage en béton avec le sculpteur Martin Wallace. D'autres matériaux, dont le granit de Lanhénin et d'autres pierres locales, affirment des liens forts entre ce bâtiment contemporain et la terre de Bretagne.

Espace des sciences

The inversion of volumes and bulbous curves seen in both images and the section to the right serve to identify the different elements of the composition, which retains a decidedly sculptural flair.

Das Eindringen von Volumen und knollenartigen Kurven – auf den beiden Abbildungen und im Schnitt rechts zu sehen – dient dazu, die verschiedenen Elemente der Komposition, die auf einem ausgeprägt skulpturalen Ansatz beruht, zu kennzeichnen.

L'inversion des volumes et les courbes bulbeuses visibles sur ces images et sur la coupe (à droite) permettent d'identifier les différents éléments de la composition qui conserve un style résolument sculptural.

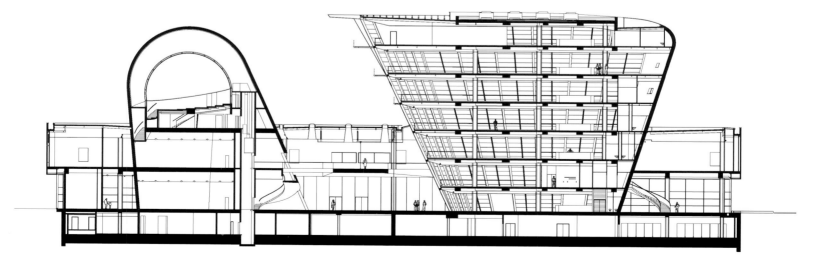

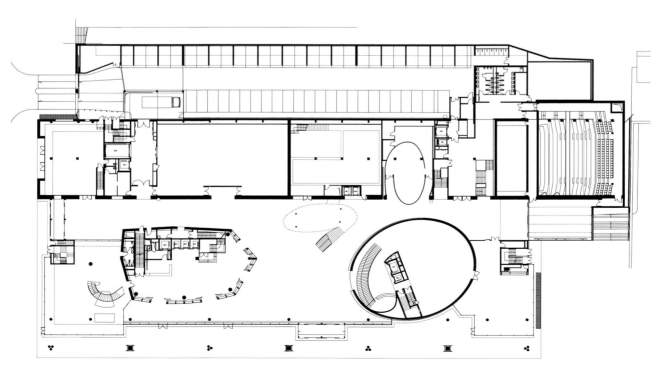

Outward leaning windows offer a panoramic view of the area around the building, while metal stairs and overhead passageways contribute to the overall impression of orchestrated complexity.

In den Außenraum gekippte Fenster ermöglichen Panoramablicke in die Umgebung; Metalltreppen und Brücken tragen zum Gesamteindruck einer orchestrierten Komplexität bei.

Les fenêtres inclinées vers l'extérieur offrent une vue panoramique sur l'environnement du bâtiment tandis que des escaliers métalliques et des passages suspendus contribuent à donner l'impression d'une complexité orchestrée.

12

RUDY RICCIOTTI

RUDY RICCIOTTI ARCHITECTE
Villa La Tartane
17, boulevard Victor Hugo
83150 Bandol

Tel: +33 4 94 29 52 61
Fax:+33 4 94 32 45 25
e-mail: rudy.ricciotti@wanadoo.fr
Web: rudyricciotti.com

Born in 1952 in Algiers, **RUDY RICCIOTTI** moved to the south of France as a child. He attended the École Supérieure Technique in Geneva, from which he graduated as an engineer in 1975, and the École d'Architecture of Marseille, from which he graduated in 1980. He founded his office in Bandol in 1980. His early work includes a number of private villas in the south of France. His first large-scale project was the Stadium in Vitrolles (1994). In 1997, he completed the College 600 secondary school in Saint-Ouen; and in 1999 a new building for the Luminy Science Faculty in Marseille. Recent work includes the Peace footbridge in Seoul, South Korea (2000); the Philharmonic Concert Hall in Potsdam, Germany (2000); the Tanzmatten concert and sports hall near Strasbourg (2001); and the Choreographic Center of Aix-en-Provence (1999–2005). Rudy Ricciotti recently won competitions for the Mucem in Marseille (European and Mediterranean Civilizations Museum, completion 2009); for the Islamic Arts' Department of the Louvre Museum in Paris (2005); and for the new building of the Venice Film Festival (2005).

NATIONAL CHOREOGRAPHIC CENTER AIX-EN-PROVENCE 1999-2005

FLOOR AREA: 2675 m²
CLIENT: City of Aix-en-Provence–SEMEPA
COST: €4.59 million

Intended as a showcase for dance in the old southern French city of Aix-en-Provence, the National Choreographic Center includes a 380-seat dance theater, four dance studios (180 m²; 130 m²; 230 m²; 100 m²), public reception spaces, backstage facilities and locker rooms for the dancers. It is the home to the Ballet Preljocaj, a reputed dance company created in 1984 that has moved frequently, most notably leaving Toulon in May 1995 when municipal elections favored the extreme right. A web of black reinforced concrete and glass, the building's unusual appearance marks the inventive presence of Ricciotti. Angelin Preljocaj describes the structure as, "Architecture of steel and concrete, whose glass skin enables the outside world to gaze upon the genesis of dance as it perfects itself day after day in the rehearsal studios, yet which retains the secret and the emotion of the performance deep within the building, in its 380-seat theater. A place for dance, where creation is buttressed from the very first rehearsals to the night of actual performance. A place, a home for the art of dance, whose constant struggle for existence has assimilated contemporary dance to a martial art. Twenty years ... is the time it has taken for this lofty vessel to take shape, to bring together the dreams, the energy, the determination and the funding."

Das Centre Choréographique National in der alten südfranzösischen Stadt Aix-en-Provence soll als Schaukasten für den Tanz dienen. Es umfasst ein Tanztheater mit 380 Sitzplätzen, vier Tanzstudios mit 100, 130, 180 und 230 m², öffentliche Empfangsräume, Bühneneinrichtungen und Garderoben für die Tänzer. Es ist feste Spielstätte des Ballet Preljocaj, einer 1984 gegründeten renommierten Tanzkompanie, die zuvor oft umzog – so ihr Weggang aus Toulon im Mai 1995, als bei den Regionalwahlen die extreme Rechte an die Macht kam. Ein Netz aus schwarzem Stahlbeton und Glas prägt das ungewöhnliche Äußere des Gebäudes und bringt Ricciottis schöpferische Haltung zum Ausdruck. Angelin Preljocaj beschreibt den Bau so: »Eine Architektur aus Stahl und Beton, deren Glashülle es der Außenwelt ermöglicht, die Entstehung von Tanz, der Tag für Tag in den Übungssälen perfektioniert wird, zu beobachten, die aber auch das Geheimnis und die Emotionen der Aufführung im Theatersaal, tief im Innern des Gebäudes, bewahrt. Ein Ort für Tanz, der die Genese von der allerersten Probe bis zur Nacht der Vorstellung unterstützt. Ein Ort, ein Zuhause für die Tanzkunst, deren beständiger Kampf um ihre Existenz den zeitgenössischen Tanz zu einer kriegerischen Kunst gemacht hat. 20 Jahre ... hat es gedauert, bis dieses luftige Gehäuse Form angenommen hat und die Träume, die Energie, die Entschlossenheit und die finanziellen Mittel beisammen waren.«

Vitrine de la danse en Aix-en-Provence, ce Centre national comprend une salle de spectacle de trois cent quatre-vingts places, quatre studios de danse (180, 130, 230, 1000 m²), des espaces pour l'accueil du public, des installations techniques et des vestiaires pour les danseurs. Le Centre est la résidence du Ballet Preljocaj, célèbre compagnie créée en 1984 qui a souvent changé de port d'attache, quittant Toulon en mai 1995 après que la mairie ait passé des accords avec l'extrême-droite. Un réseau de poutres de béton armé noir et de panneaux de verre donne un aspect étrange à ce bâtiment qui signale fortement l'intervention créative de Ricciotti. Pour Angelin Preljocaj, « [le Centre] est une structure en béton et acier dont la peau de verre permet au monde extérieur de voir la genèse de la danse qui se perfectionne jour après jour dans les studios de répétition, tout en conservant le secret et l'émotion du spectacle au plus profond du bâtiment... Un lieu pour la danse, où la création est soutenue dès les premières répétitions et jusqu'à la soirée du spectacle-même. Un lieu, un foyer pour cet art dont le combat constant pour exister a fait assimiler la danse contemporaine à un art martial. Vingt ans... c'est le temps qu'il a fallu pour que ce vaisseau aérien prenne forme, pour réunir les rêves, l'énergie, la détermination et les financements. »

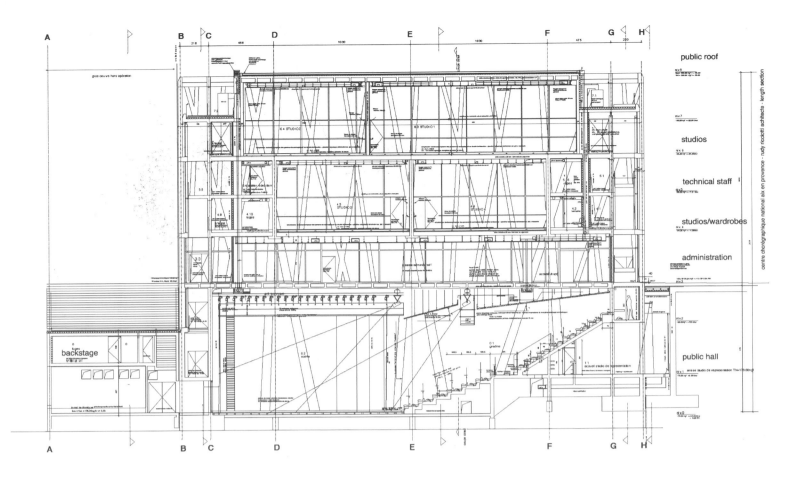

public roof

studios

technical staff

studios/wardrobes

administration

public hall

backstage

The blackened exterior of the structure might bring to mind an incomplete building in these pictures taken before the inauguration, but Ricciotti is clearly seeking to challenge conventional wisdom, particularly as a cultural facility.

Diese äußere Struktur des Gebäudes mag an ein unvollendetes Bauwerk erinnern wie hier auf den Fotos während der Bauzeit. Ricciotti fordert damit konventionelle Vorstellungen heraus, besonders im Zusammenhang mit einer kulturellen Einrichtung.

L'extérieur noir pourrait évoquer une construction inachevée dans ces images prises avant l'inauguration, mais Ricciotti adore provoquer, en particulier dans le contexte d'un équipement culturel.

VALODE & PISTRE

13

VALODE & PISTRE ARCHITECTES
115, rue du Bac
75007 Paris

Tel: +33 1 53 63 22 00
Fax: +33 1 53 63 22 09
e-mail: info@valode-et-pistre.com
Web: www.valode-et-pistre.com

Opus 12 Tower (left building)

DENIS VALODE was born in 1946. He received his architecture degree in 1969 from the École des Beaux-Arts in Paris and taught there from 1970 to 1985. JEAN PISTRE was born in 1951 and also studied architecture at the École des Beaux-Arts in Paris, graduating in 1974. The two men first worked together in 1977 and created Valode & Pistre in 1980. Today the office employs up to 200 persons and provides interior, architectural and urban design as well as engineering services. Built work in France includes the renovation of the Museum for Contemporary Art (CAPC) in Bordeaux (1990); Shell Headquarters, Reuil-Malmaison (1988–91); L'Oréal factory in Aulnay-sous-Bois (1992); installation of the Direction régionale des Affaires Culturelles (Regional Cultural Authority) in an 18th-century building in Lyon (1987–92); Leonardo da Vinci University in Courbevoie (1992–95); and Air France Headquarters at Roissy Airport (1992–95). Recent work includes the renovation of 19th-century warehouses in Bercy, Paris, into a modern commercial area (1998–2001); the Cap Gemini Ernst & Young campus in Gouvieux (2002); the master plan and buildings for the Renault Technocentre in Guyancourt near Paris (completed in 2003); and the Opus 12 office tower renovation at La Défense (2002). Valode & Pistre are currently working on the reconstruction of the Beaugrenelle shopping center in Paris; a group of buildings at Jiuxianqiao (Beijing, China); a 250-room Hyatt Hotel (Ekaterinburg, Russia); a hotel, residential and office complex at the Graving Docks (Glasgow, Scotland); and the new T1 Tower at La Défense.

OPUS 12 OFFICE TOWER LA DEFENSE
PARIS 2000 - 02

FLOOR AREA: 36 000 m²
CLIENT: AXA Insurance
COST: not disclosed

The architects were called on to rebuild the Crédit Lyonnais Tower erected in 1970 on the southern side of the Défense area of Paris. The building owner, the large insurance company AXA, first determined that demolishing the existing tower would be prohibitively expensive and then organized a competition in which the Miami firm Arquitectonica and others participated. Encumbered by an unsightly load-bearing façade with pillars set every 1.4 meters, the old tower was completely rebuilt by Valode & Pistre, and every story was enlarged by 200 m² in the process. Since local building regulations do not allow an increase in total floor area, the architects dug into little-used underground spaces, reducing floor space in the lower levels, but bringing light into the areas below grade. This relatively simple gesture allowed them to increase average floor size from 800 m² to 1000 m² in the parts of the building above ground, currently considered an ideal size on the Paris real estate market. The approach of Valode & Pistre involved creating a new superstructure outside the walls of the old building, driving beams into its core to create a new support system and then progressively demolishing the old load-bearing façade from the top down. The new semireflective glass façade was then put in place from the bottom up. The architects estimate that the cost of this complex operation was 10 to 15% higher than new construction, but since it avoided expensive demolition, it met the client's needs.

Die Architekten waren aufgefordert, den 1970 errichteten Büroturm der Crédit Lyonnais auf der Südseite von La Défense in Paris umzubauen. Der Eigentümer, die große Versicherungsgesellschaft AXA, hatte errechnet, dass ein Abriss des Turms exorbitant hohe Kosten verursachen würde, und einen Wettbewerb ausgeschrieben, an dem u. a. Arquitectonica aus Miami teilnahm. Das Hochhaus, das durch eine unansehnliche tragende Fassade mit einem Stützabstand von 1,4 m belastet war, wurde komplett saniert und zudem die Grundfläche jedes Geschosses um 200 m² vergrößert. Da aufgrund der örtlichen Baubestimmungen eine Vergrößerung der Gesamtfläche nicht zulässig war, reduzierten Valode & Pistre wenig genutzte Flächen in den Untergeschossen und verbesserten die Belichtung dieser Bereiche. Mit dieser relativ einfachen Geste konnte die durchschnittliche Geschossfläche in den Obergeschossen von 800 m² auf 1000 m² erhöht werden, was auf dem Pariser Immobilienmarkt derzeit als ideale Größe gilt. Der Vorschlag von Valode & Pistre beinhaltete u. a. die Konstruktion einer neuen Glashülle für das alte Gebäude, das Ansetzen neuer Träger an den Gebäudekernen zur Schaffung eines neuen Tragsystems und den sukzessiven Rückbau der vorhandenen tragenden Fassade von oben nach unten. Die Architekten schätzen, dass die Kosten für diese komplexe Operation 10 bis 15 % höher lagen als für einen Neubau, so konnten aber auch ohne Abriss die Forderungen des Bauherrn erfüllt werden.

Les architectes ont été appelés pour reconstruire une tour du Crédit Lyonnais édifiée en 1970 dans la partie sud du quartier de La Défense. Le propriétaire, l'importante compagnie d'assurances AXA, après avoir constaté que la démolition de la tour serait extraordinairement coûteuse, avait décidé d'organiser un concours auquel participa, entre autres, l'agence Arquitectonica de Miami. Encombrée d'une façade porteuse et peu avenante rythmée par des piliers tous les mètres et demi, l'ancienne tour fut entièrement reprise par Valode & Pistre qui ont agrandi chaque niveau de 200 m². Comme la réglementation de La Défense interdit d'augmenter la surface totale d'un immeuble, les architectes ont réduit des espaces souterrains peu utilisés, y apportant de la lumière tout en gagnant des mètres carrés. Ce geste relativement simple leur a permis d'accroître la surface de chaque niveau au-dessus du sol de 800 à 1000 m² afin d'atteindre des dimensions correspondant au marché de l'immobilier parisien. Cette solution a entraîné la création d'une nouvelle superstructure en avant des murs existants – des poutres partant du noyau pour créer un nouveau système porteur – puis en démolissant progressivement l'ancienne façade porteuse à partir du haut. La nouvelle façade en verre semi-réfléchissant fut ensuite mise en place à partir du bas. Les architectes estiment que le coût de cette opération complexe a été de 10% à 15% plus élevé que celui d'une construction neuve, mais elle évitait les énormes frais d'une démolition complète.

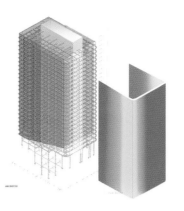

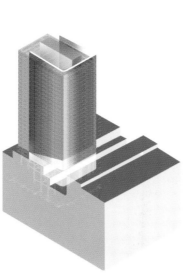

The outdated design of the former tower was overhauled in a spectacular way by the architects, who completely changed the façade and added to existing floor space, while digging into the ground to bring light to formerly little-used areas below grade.

Die aus der Mode gekommene ursprüngliche Gestaltung des Hochhauses wurde auf spektakuläre Weise erneuert. Die Architekten veränderten die Fassade komplett, vergrößerten die Geschossflächen und gruben ein Atrium in den Boden, um Licht in die vormals wenig genutzten Flächen in den Untergeschossen zu bringen.

Le style démodé de la tour d'origine a été transformé de manière spectaculaire par les architectes. Ils ont complètement changé la façade et ont accru la surface de chaque niveau en creusant en profondeur pour apporter la lumière dans des zones de sous-sol jusqu'alors peu utilisées.

The tower formerly had a façade that was identical on all sides. To differentiate the surfaces of the new towers, the architects studied the location and factors such as solar-heat gain. Their ingenious method consisted in driving supports into the core of the building and then dismantling the load-bearing façade before adding a new skin and extra floor space.

Ursprünglich hatte der Turm vier gleiche Seiten. Die Architekten untersuchten den Standort und Faktoren wie die Aufheizung durch Sonneneinstrahlung, um die neuen Oberflächen zu differenzieren. Durch neue Träger, die in den Gebäudekern eingelassen wurden, konnte die tragende Fassade abgebaut, die Geschossfläche vergrößert und eine neue Gebäudehülle installiert werden.

Alors que l'ancienne tour présentait des façades toutes identiques, les architectes ont étudié l'orientation et des facteurs comme la chaleur solaire pour les différencier. Leur méthode de transformation a consisté à installer un nouveau système porteur à partir du noyau de l'immeuble puis à démonter l'ancienne façade porteuse avant d'ajouter une nouvelle peau et d'agrandir les niveaux.

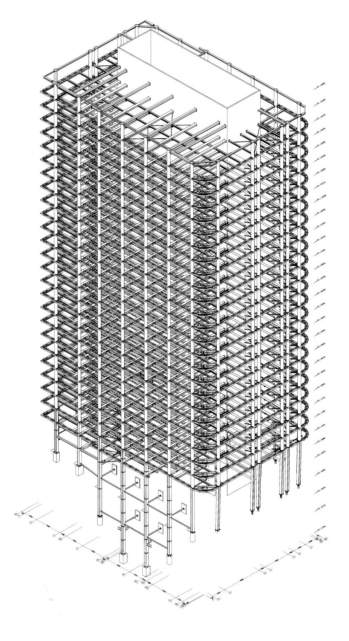

Typical of the architects is the combination of rather dense metallic elements, such as the stairways seen to the left, and smooth black-and-white surfaces, as in the image above.

Typisch für die Architekten ist die Kombination von eher dichten Bauteilen aus Metall – z. B. die Treppe links – mit glatten schwarzen und weißen Oberflächen wie im Bild oben.

Selon leur habitude, les architectes combinent des éléments en métal assez présents, comme les escaliers (à gauche), et des plans lisses blancs et noirs comme dans l'image ci-dessus.

CAP GEMINI / ERNST & YOUNG UNIVERSITY

GOUVIEUX 2000 - 02

FLOOR AREA: 23 000 m²
CLIENT: Cap Gemini / Ernst & Young
COST: not disclosed

With 90 000 employees spread all over the world Cap Gemini/Ernst & Young decided to create a seminar facility in France. They selected a 50-hectare site in Gouvieux, not far from Paris and close to Chantilly Palace. A 19th-century palace built on the site by the Rothschild family became a central element in the composition envisaged by Valode & Pistre. Setting a low, semicircular building directly opposite the old structure, which was entirely restored by them, the architects succeeded in providing the client with the image of French tradition that they were looking for while adding seminar rooms, lodging and leisure facilities in a clearly modern style. French garden design as well as the work of Edwin Lutyens influenced the architects, but above all, they showed a capacity to blend old and new in a convincing fashion that avoids any hint of postmodern pastiche. Despite dealing frequently with large corporate clients like Cap Gemini/Ernst & Young, Valode & Pistre retain a sensitivity to site and function that allows them to modernize even the "Disney-like" castle in the center of this composition.

Cap Gemini/Ernst & Young, ein Unternehmen mit weltweit 90 000 Angestellten, beschloss den Bau eines Seminargebäudes in Frankreich. Man entschied sich für ein 50 ha großes Grundstück in Gouvieux, nicht weit von Paris und in der Nähe des Schlosses Chantilly gelegen. Ein Anwesen der Familie Rothschild aus dem 19. Jahrhundert bildet das zentrale Element in dem Ensemble von Valode & Pistre. Indem sie dem von ihnen komplett sanierten Schlossbau ein flaches, halbkreisförmiges Gebäude direkt gegenüberstellten, gelang es den Architekten, das vom Bauherrn gewünschte Bild französischer Tradition zu transportieren und gleichzeitig in einer klaren und modernen Sprache Seminarräume, Gästezimmer und Freizeiteinrichtungen vorzusehen. Einflüsse französischer Gartenplanungen und der Entwürfe Edwin Lutyens sind erkennbar, vor allem aber bewiesen die Architekten die Fähigkeit, Altes und Neues auf überzeugende Art miteinander zu verbinden und postmodernes Nachahmen gänzlich zu vermeiden. Obwohl Valode & Pistre häufig für große Bauherrn wie Cap Gemini/Ernst & Young arbeiten, haben sie sich einen sensiblen Umgang mit dem Grundstück und der Funktion bewahrt, der es ihnen erlaubt, auch ein Schloss im Stil des verspielten Eklektizismus im Mittelpunkt eines Ensembles zu modernisieren.

Du fait qu'elle emploie plus de 90 000 personnes dans le monde entier, la société Cap Gemini/Ernst & Young avait décidé de créer en France des installations pour séminaires. Un terrain de cinquante hectares fut choisi non loin de Paris, à Gouvieux près du château de Chantilly. Un château du XIXᵉ siècle construit pour la famille Rothschild constitue l'élément central de la composition imaginée par Valode & Pistre. En implantant un bâtiment bas et semi-circulaire directement face à l'ancienne résidence entièrement restaurée par leurs soins, les architectes ont réussi à conserver, selon le désir du client, l'image d'une certaine tradition française, tout en logeant des installations de séminaires, d'hébergement et de loisirs, traitées dans un style résolument moderne. Les principes du jardin à la française et les travaux de l'architecte Edwin Lutyens les ont certes inspirés, mais ils ont avant tout montré leur capacité à associer l'ancien et le neuf d'une façon convaincante, sans la moindre dérive vers le pastiche postmoderniste. Tout en travaillant fréquemment pour d'importants clients institutionnels comme Cap Gemini/Ernst & Young, Valode & Pistre ont su conserver cette sensibilité aux sites et aux fonctions qui leur a même permis de moderniser le château de style éclectique qui est au centre de leur composition.

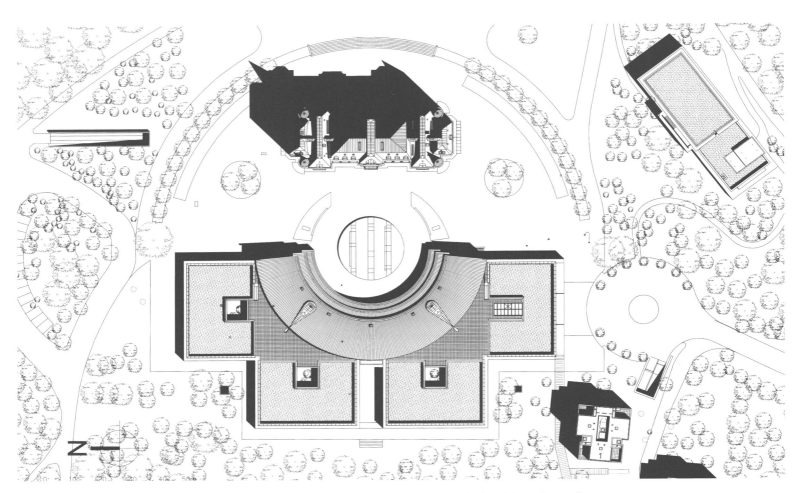

The site plan above shows how the new structure, a composition made of a semicircle and rectangles, faces and responds to the existing palace. Elevations below emphasize the low-lying design intended not to compete unduly with the old architecture.

Der Lageplan mit dem Neubau, einer Komposition aus einem Halbkreis und Rechtecken, die dem alten Schlossgebäude gegenübersteht. Die Ansichten zeigen den niedrigen Neubau, der nicht mit der vorhandenen Architektur konkurrieren soll.

Le plan du site (ci-dessus) montre la nouvelle structure, une composition en demi-cercles et rectangles qui fait face au château. Les élévations (ci-dessous) soulignent la discrétion du projet qui évite d'entrer inutilement en concurrence avec l'architecture ancienne.

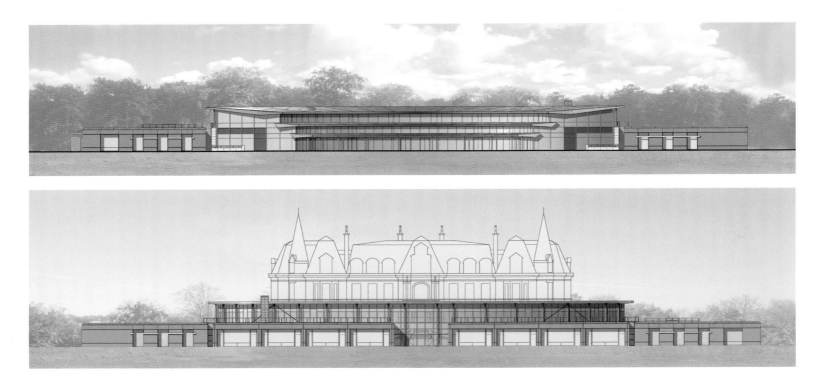

The existing palace was completely renovated by the architects. The image above again shows how the new buildings lie well below the roof line of the palace.

Das alte Schlossgebäude wurde vollständig saniert. Die Höhe des Neubaus liegt deutlich unterhalb der Linie des Schlossdaches.

Le château a été entièrement rénové par les architectes. L'image ci-dessus montre que la hauteur des nouveaux bâtiments reste bien en deçà de la ligne de faîte du château.

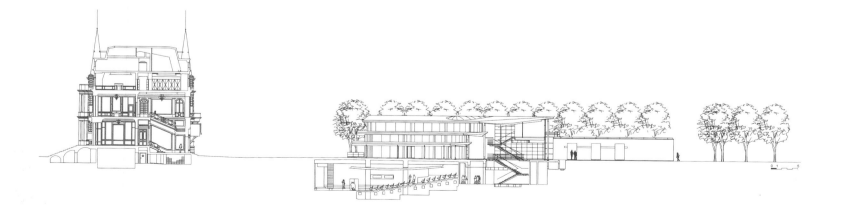

The sophisticated modernism of Valode & Pistre stands opposite the "neo" style of the former Rothschild château. Details such as the columns seen above were very carefully studied by the architects, giving an overall impression of fine workmanship.

Valode & Pistres anspruchsvoller Modernismus bildet einen Gegensatz zum »Neo«-Stil des ehemaligen Rothschild-Schlosses. Details wie die Stützen im Bild oben wurden sorgfältig entworfen und vermitteln insgesamt den Eindruck von solidem Handwerk.

Le modernisme sophistiqué de Valode & Pistre s'oppose au style « néo » de l'ancien château Rothschild. Des détails tels que les colonnes ci-dessus ont été soigneusement étudiés pour donner le sentiment d'un ensemble aux finitions très minutieuses.

A double staircase that might well echo French tradition gives a certain visual complexity to an otherwise "smooth" environment. The architects are acutely conscious not only of the function of their building, but also of the client's desire for a feeling of "rootedness" in a French environment.

Eine doppelte Treppe erinnert an französische Bautradition und verleiht dem ansonsten »glatten« Ambiente eine gewisse visuelle Komplexität. Die Architekten achten nicht nur auf die funktionalen Anforderungen an das Gebäude, sie berücksichtigen auch den Wunsch des Bauherrn nach einer Verwurzelung in einem französischen Ambiente.

L'escalier double, clin d'œil à la tradition française, confère une certaine complexité visuelle à un environnement par ailleurs assez « lisse ». Les architectes étaient très conscients non seulement de la fonction du projet mais aussi du souhait du client d'inscrire celui-ci dans un environnement « authentiquement » français.

#14

JEAN-PAUL VIGUIER

JEAN-PAUL VIGUIER
S.A. D'ARCHITECTURE
16, rue du Champ de l'Alouette
75013 Paris

Tel: +33 1 44 08 62 00
Fax: +33 1 44 08 62 02
e-mail: jpviguier@viguier.com
Web: www.viguier.com

Born in 1946 in Azas, **JEAN-PAUL VIGUIER** studied architecture at the École des Beaux-Arts and graduated in 1970. In 1971, he received a fellowship to study city planning at Harvard, where he obtained his Master's degree in 1973. Back in France, he founded his first company, Jean-Paul Viguier, Jean-François Jodry et Associés, in 1974. Their major works were Metropole 19 industrial workshops, Paris (1986–87), and the André Citroën Park, Paris (1992). In 1992, Viguier founded his own agency, which now has a staff of 60 people. Their main built work includes the Cœur Défense towers, Paris (1992–2001); France Television headquarters, Paris (1994–98); a large commercial center, Meulun Sénart (1997–2002); the Mediatheque Cathedrale, Reims (1997–2003); the Water Tower Hotel, Chicago (1998–2002); and the French ministry of sports, Paris (2004). Jean-Paul Viguier is currently building the Natural History Museum, Toulouse (2000–06); the new wing of the MacNay Museum, San Antonio, Texas (2002–06); the Castres Hospital, France (2002–08); and a mixed-use building on the Vörösmarty Plaza in the center of Budapest (2003–06).

MUSEUM OF NATURAL HISTORY
TOULOUSE
2000 - 07

FLOOR AREA: 3700 m² (renovation) and 5800 m² (new construction)
CLIENT: Ville de Toulouse, Musée d'Histoire Naturelle
de Toulouse (director: Jean-François Lapeyre)
COST: €15 million (construction) and €5 million (museum design)
PROJECT DIRECTOR: Bertrand Beaussillon
MUSEOLOGIST: Xavier Leroux-Cauche
SUPERVISING ARCHITECT ON SITE: Xavier Ratinsky, LCR, Toulouse

Jean-Paul Viguier's mission was to create a new, unified entity out of the three parts of this project: the rehabilitation of an existing structure (3700 m²), the construction of a new building (5800 m²) directly connected to the old museum and the design for a botanical garden. Jean-Paul Viguier was also given responsibility for the museum design. The new building consists essentially of two large unencumbered exhibition floors, while activities and information services are concentrated in the old building. A 120-meter-long curved glass façade is intended as the architectural element linking the old, the new and the botanical garden. The sober, horizontal design of this new part of the museum is meant to allow the old building and the neighboring church to continue to play their roles in the urban environment. Insofar as the museum design is concerned, Viguier wanted to separate actual objects of historic value from ones conceived as evocations of natural history, thus breaking somewhat with French tradition in this area. He also felt that it is important to "tease" the visitor by not unveiling the whole scheme too quickly, thus inciting visitors to explore the entire exhibition. Like the museum itself, which makes use of an existing structure, the garden is designed around specimens planted earlier. The resulting 365-meter-long "spiral" follows a small stream and is conceived as a "journey of initiation."

Jean-Paul Viguiers Aufgabe bestand darin, aus den drei Teilen des Projekts – der Sanierung des vorhandenen Museums (3700 m²), einem damit direkt verbundenen Neubau (5800 m²) und einem neuen botanischen Garten – ein einheitliches Ganzes zu machen. Auch die Ausstellungsarchitektur wurde dem Architekten übertragen. Das neue Gebäude besteht im Wesentlichen aus zwei Ausstellungsebenen ohne störende Nebennutzungen; Räume für besondere Aktivitäten und Informationsdienste sind im alten Gebäude untergebracht. Eine 120 m lange gekrümmte Glasfassade verbindet als architektonisches Element das Alte, das Neue und den botanischen Garten. Die nüchterne, horizontal betonte Architektur dieses Elements soll es dem alten Gebäude und der benachbarten Kirche erlauben, auch weiterhin ihre Rolle im städtischen Kontext zu spielen. Bei der Ausstellungsarchitektur ging es Viguier darum, die historisch wertvollen Ausstellungsstücke von den Objekten, die Teile von naturkundlichen Szenarien sind, klar zu trennen. Dadurch bricht er in gewisser Weise mit tradierten französischen Vorstellungen in diesem Bereich. Außerdem war es ihm wichtig, den Besucher etwas an der Nase herumzuführen, indem das Gesamtkonzept nicht zu schnell erfasst werden kann und der Besucher so dazu animiert wird, seinen Besuch nicht auf halbem Weg abzubrechen. Wie das Museum, das ein bestehendes Gebäude mitnutzt, wurde der botanische Garten um bereits vorhandene Pflanzen herum angelegt. Die so geschaffene 365 m lange Spirale folgt einem kleinen Bach und ist als »Reise zum Beginn« gedacht.

La mission de Jean-Paul Viguier était de créer une entité unifiée à partir du triple programme de ce projet : la réhabilitation d'une construction existante de 3700 m², la construction d'un nouveau bâtiment de 5800 m² directement connecté à l'ancien musée et la conception d'un jardin botanique. L'architecte était également chargé de l'aménagement intérieur du musée. Le bâtiment neuf comprend essentiellement deux vastes niveaux dégagés, tandis que les services et les activités sont réunis dans le bâtiment ancien. Une façade en verre incurvée de cent vingt mètres de long relie l'ancienne construction, la nouvelle et le jardin botanique. Les lignes sobres et l'horizontalité de cette nouvelle partie du musée préservent la place de l'ancien bâtiment et de l'église voisine dans le contexte urbain. Pour l'aménagement intérieur, Viguier a voulu clairement séparer les objets « historiques » de ceux utilisés pour évoquer l'histoire naturelle, rompant ainsi en partie avec la tradition muséale en vigueur dans ce domaine. Il a également pensé qu'il était important de stimuler la curiosité du visiteur en ne révélant pas trop vite le contenu des expositions pour l'inciter à aller jusqu'au bout de la visite. De même que le musée utilise une structure préexistante, la conception du jardin a tenu compte des essences en place depuis longtemps. La « spirale » de 365 m de long qu'il dessine suit un petit ruisseau et est conçue comme un « parcours d'initiation ».

Curving and well integrated into its environment, the new building lies below the old and is part of the botanic garden design in which the architect was also involved.

Gekurvt und in seine Umgebung eingebettet, liegt der Neubau unterhalb des vorhandenen Gebäudes und bildet mit dem botanischen Garten, an dessen Entwurf der Architekt ebenfalls beteiligt war, eine Einheit.

Incurvé et inséré avec franchise dans son environnement, le nouveau bâtiment est situé sous l'ancien et s'intègre au jardin botanique, à la conception duquel l'architecte a également participé.

Images and the plan to the right show the architect's obvious intention: to unify the otherwise somewhat disparate elements of the museum into a coherent whole. Viguier shows a sensitivity to context and an ability to integrate modern forms into a problematic old setting.

Die Abbildungen und der Grundriss zeigen deutlich die Intention, aus den sehr unterschiedlichen Elementen des Museums ein einheitliches Ganzes zu bilden. Mit Sensibilität führt Viguier moderne Formen in ein problematisches Ensemble ein.

Les images et le plan de droite montrent l'intention évidente d'unifier les éléments assez disparates du musée pour en faire un ensemble cohérent. Viguier a montré ici sa sensibilité au contexte et son habileté à intégrer des formes modernes dans un cadre ancien.

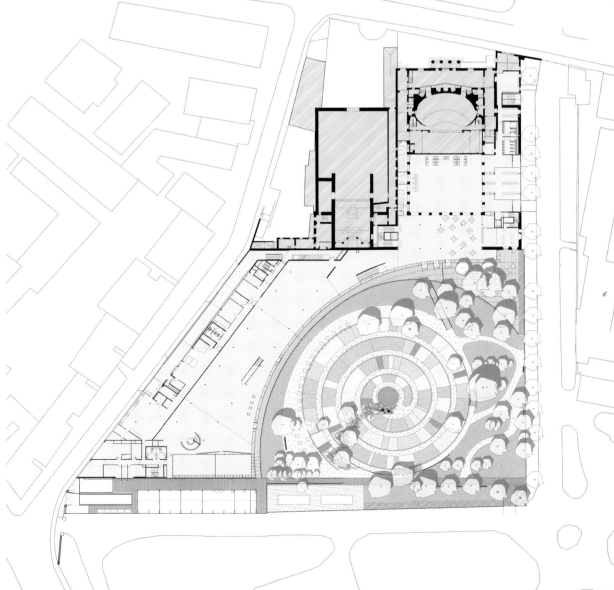

15

JEAN-MICHEL WILMOTTE

**WILMOTTE ET ASSOCIÉS
SA D'ARCHITECTURE**
68, rue du Faubourg Saint-Antoine
75012 Paris

Tel: +33 1 53 02 22 22
Fax: +33 1 43 44 17 11
e-mail: wilmotte@wilmotte.fr
Web: www.wilmotte.com

Born in 1948, a graduate of the Camondo School in Paris, JEAN-MICHEL WILMOTTE formed his own firm in 1975. Although he is best known as an interior designer, Wilmotte joined the Order of Architects in France in 1993. With approximately 114 employees, his office has worked on urban furniture design in Lyon, Bordeaux, Thionville and Orléans, as well as in Italy (Milan, Latina) and in Russia (design of the central quai of the Volgograd, 2005). He has also designed urban furniture for the Champs-Élysées in Paris and for the avenue de France. He has been able to make use of the experience he gathered as architect of the Decorative Arts Department of the Louvre in the Richelieu wing, completed in 1993, on numerous cultural institutions. He completed museum design projects for the Musée des Beaux-Arts de Lyon (1991–98); the Chiado Museum, Lisbon (1994); the Musée National du Liban, Beirut (1999); and San Domenico in Forli, Italy (2005). Jean-Michel Wilmotte designed two buildings in Tokyo, the International Executive Office building in the Shinjuku area and the New N°3 Arai building, as well as the Gana Art Center, Seoul (1996–98) and a museum for objects given to French President Jacques Chirac in Saran, France. Recent work includes the design of a new boutique concept for Cartier in Paris, Milan, New York, Los Angeles and Tokyo (2000) as well as the construction of offices, hotels and residences near the station in Antwerp. He has also worked recently on new showrooms for Chaumet, John Galliano and Montblanc International; interior design of the LVMH Headquarters, Paris; as well as numerous housing, cultural or rehabilitation projects in France, Italy and Korea. He is currently completing the interior design of the Museum of Islamic Arts, Doha, Qatar (architect: I. M. Pei) and of the Rijksmuseum, Amsterdam. His reputation for cultural facilities has also led him to work on the Centre National du Costume de Scène (National Center for Theater Costumes), located in Moulins, France, and the Museum of Jewish Art in Brussels. In 2005, he created the Wilmotte Foundation to encourage European architectural culture and to create communication between architecture, the preservation of historic heritage and contemporary design. In 2006, he gave the first "W Award" for young talents.

FREJUS ST RAPHAËL COMMUNITY THEATER

FREJUS 2006-08

FLOOR AREA: 5375 m²
CLIENT: Communauté d'Agglomération
Fréjus St-Raphaël
COST: €11.9 million

Julius Cesar and the Roman emperor Augustus gave great importance to the coastal town of Fréjus, fortifying it, building a port and market, and laying out two major axes, the Decumanus Maximus (northeast/southeast) and the Cardo Maximus (northwest/southeast). The new Fréjus Theater is located at the intersection of these two historic roads. The 75-meter-long, 40 large and 18-meter high elliptical building "recalls Roman arenas and theaters," according to the architect. Its positioning and layout are compatible with those of the original Roman buildings of the city. The theater is to include a flexible 830-seat theater and a 150-seat naturally lit facility for rehearsals. It is to be used for dance, music and theater and thus has to provide for very different kinds of stage requirements. A canopy marks the entrance and a lobby can be used for exhibitions and receptions. Parking for 233 vehicles is part of the project, as are two levels of office space. Elliptical and compact, the architecture is intended to offer a variety of different types of space, ranging from the behind-the-scenes areas indispensable to a theater, located at the rear of the ellipse, and the more open, public spaces that make the facility inviting for the public. Both truck delivery at the rear and public access at the front are at ground level, making access to the theater particularly easy.

Julius Cäsar und der römische Kaiser Augustus maßen der Küstenstadt Fréjus eine hohe Bedeutung zu; sie befestigten sie, bauten einen Hafen sowie einen Markt und legten zwei Hauptachsen an, den Decumanus Maximus (Nordost/Südwest) und den Cardo Maximus (Nordwest/Südost). Der neue Theaterbau befindet sich an der Kreuzung dieser beiden historischen Straßen. Das 75 m lange, 40 m tiefe und 18 m hohe elliptische Gebäude »erinnert an römische Arenen und Theater«, so der Architekt. Seine Positionierung und Anlage stehen mit denen der historischen römischen Gebäude in der Stadt in Einklang. Im Theater wird es einen flexiblen Saal mit 860 Sitzplätzen und einen natürlich belichteten Probesaal mit 200 Sitzplätzen geben. Aufgrund der Nutzung für Tanz-, Musik- und Theatervorführungen muss der Bau sehr verschiedenen Arten von Bühnenanforderungen gerecht werden. Ein Vordach markiert den Eingang; in der Lobby können Ausstellungen und Empfänge stattfinden. Weiterhin umfasst das Projekt 220 Parkplätze sowie Büroräume auf zwei Geschossen. Der elliptische und kompakte Bau wird eine Reihe von unterschiedlichen Raumtypen anbieten: von dem unentbehrlichen Backstagebereich im hinteren Teil der Ellipse bis zu den offeneren öffentlichen Bereichen für das Publikum. Sowohl die Anlieferung für Lkw im hinteren Bereich als auch der öffentliche Zugang vorne befinden sich auf Erdgeschossniveau und ermöglichen eine besonders einfache Erschließung des Gebäudes.

Jules César et l'empereur Auguste accordèrent une grande importance à la ville côtière de Fréjus, la fortifiant et la dotant d'un port et d'un marché. Le nouveau théâtre se trouve d'ailleurs au carrefour de deux anciens axes romains, le Decumanus maximus et le Cardo maximus. Sa masse elliptique de 75 mètres de long sur 40 de large et 18 de haut rappelle, selon l'architecte, « les arènes et théâtres romains ». Son positionnement et son plan correspondent à ceux de constructions de la ville antique. Le théâtre contiendra une salle de spectacle modulable de huit cent soixante places et une autre de deux cents places, à éclairage naturel, pour les répétitions. Sa programmation qui repose sur la danse, la musique et le théâtre, implique des installations scéniques particulières. Un auvent signale l'entrée et le foyer pourra être utilisé pour des expositions et des réceptions. Un parking de deux cent vingt places fait partie du projet, ainsi que deux niveaux de bureaux. Elliptique et compacte à la fois, l'architecture permet l'aménagement de divers types d'espaces, notamment les coulisses techniques situées au fond de l'ellipse et des espaces publics accueillants. Les accès en rez-de-chaussée, aussi bien pour le public à l'avant que les livraisons à l'arrière, rendent le fonctionnement de ce théâtre particulièrement efficace.

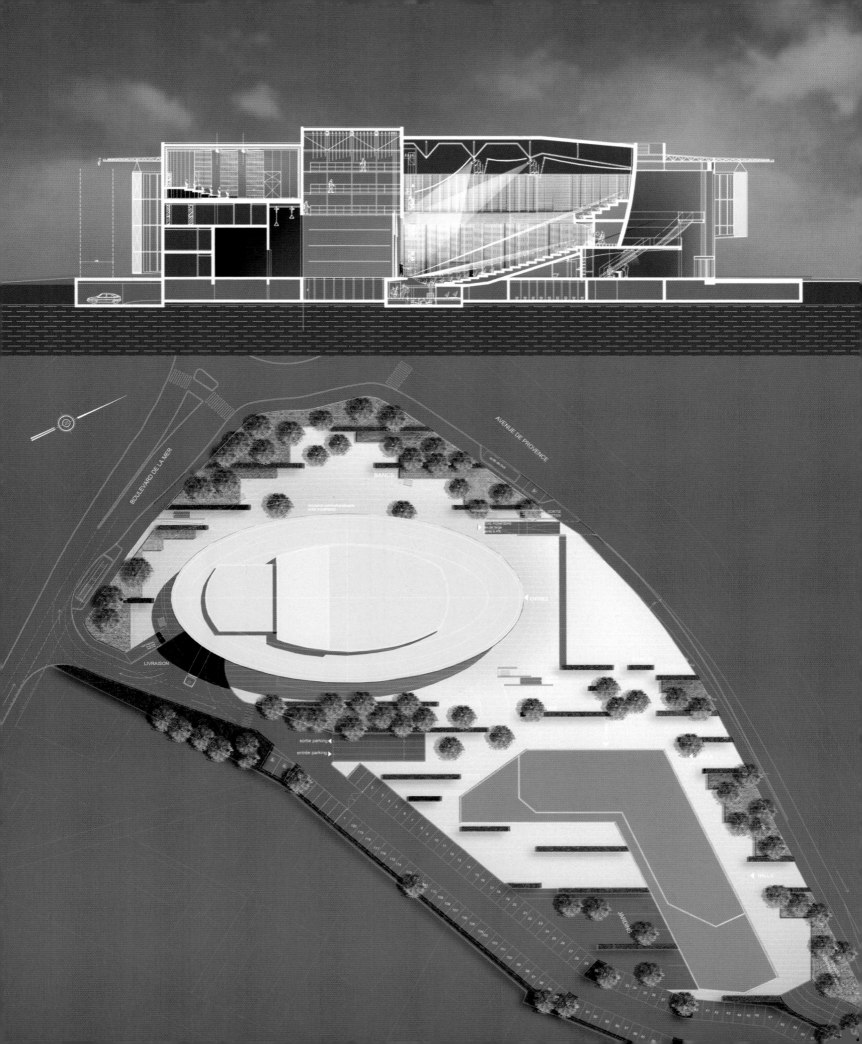

TOUR DU RUOU HOUSE
FLAYOSC
2003 - 05

FLOOR AREA: 202 m²
CLIENT: not disclosed
COST: not disclosed

Working as he has on other occasions with the talented landscape architect Jean Mus, Jean-Michel Wilmotte rehabilitated an abandoned 1970s modernist house. The architect's goal was to render the house more functional and habitable than it had been originally. He added some openings and did away with others. A ceiling window was added to bring more light into the interior, while the usual technical matters such as water, electricity, heating and insulation were dealt with in an efficient and unobtrusive manner. As the architect says, the new façade is "more ordered and silent" than was the original one. In Wilmotte's typical style, a simpler, purer geometry was imposed on the house. The extension to the house was dealt with in materials that recall the style of the earlier house as well as local finishes. The plot of land was left much as it was, with some effort expended on stabilizing the inclined entrance path. Wilmotte is at his best when working on this type of rehabilitation, remaining close to the spirit of the place while rendering it modern and more efficient.

Wie auch schon bei anderen Projekten arbeitete Jean-Michel Wilmotte bei der Instandsetzung des der Moderne verpflichteten Hauses aus den 1970er Jahren mit dem begabten Landschaftsarchitekten Jean Mus zusammen. Intention des Architekten war es, das Haus funktionaler und wohnlicher zu machen als es ursprünglich war. Einige Öffnungen kamen hinzu, andere wurden geschlossen; ein neues Oberlicht verbessert die Belichtung im Inneren des Hauses. Die übliche haustechnische Versorgung mit Wasser, Elektrizität und Heizung sowie die Dämmung sind effizient und unauffällig. Wie der Architekt sagt, ist die neue Fassade »geordneter und stiller« als zuvor. Das Haus zeigt jetzt die für Wilmotte typische einfachere, reinere Geometrie. Für den Anbau wurden Materialien verwendet, die sich auf die Architektur des vorhandenen Hauses und auf die für die Region charakteristischen Oberflächen beziehen. Das Grundstück blieb weitgehend unverändert, der Zugangsweg, der eine Steigung aufweist, wurde stabilisiert. Indem er sich eng an den »Genius Loci« hält und ihn modern und effizient interpretiert, zeigt sich Wilmotte bei dieser Art von Instandsetzung von seiner besten Seite.

Travaillant, comme en de multiples occasions, avec le talentueux architecte paysagiste Jean Mus, Jean-Michel Wilmotte a réhabilité ici une maison de style moderniste des années 1970. Son objectif était de la rendre plus fonctionnelle et habitable qu'elle ne l'était à l'origine. Il a ajouté quelques ouvertures et en a supprimé d'autres. Une verrière zénithale apporte davantage de lumière à l'intérieur et les aspects techniques – eau, électricité, chauffage et isolation – ont été traités de façon efficace et discrète. La nouvelle façade est « plus ordonnée et plus silencieuse » que la précédente, selon Wilmotte, qui a appliqué à cette maison une géométrie plus simple et plus pure, caractéristique du style de l'architecte. L'extension a été traitée dans des matériaux qui rappellent le style antérieur mais aussi les pratiques constructives locales. La parcelle de terrain a été laissée en grande partie telle quelle, même s'il a fallu stabiliser le terrain incliné du chemin d'accès. Wilmotte est au sommet de son art dans ce type de réhabilitation, où il sait rester proche de l'esprit du lieu tout en mettant l'accent sur la modernité et l'efficacité.

6/2015
10